WINE DOGS
AUSTRALIA
— 3 —

more dogs from Australian wineries

Craig McGill and Susan Elliott

A Giant Dog book

WINE DOGS® IS A REGISTERED TRADEMARK

WINE DOGS AUSTRALIA 3
MORE DOGS FROM AUSTRALIAN WINERIES

ISBN 978-1-921336-28-7

COPYRIGHT © GIANT DOG, FIRST EDITION 2012
WINE DOGS® IS A REGISTERED TRADEMARK

DESIGNED BY SUSAN ELLIOTT, COPYRIGHT © McGILL DESIGN GROUP PTY LTD, 2012
ALL ILLUSTRATIONS COPYRIGHT © CRAIG McGILL, McGILL DESIGN GROUP PTY LTD, 2012
ALL TEXT NOT ATTRIBUTED, COPYRIGHT © CRAIG McGILL, McGILL DESIGN GROUP PTY LTD, 2012

ALL PHOTOGRAPHY © CRAIG McGILL, 2012 WITH THE EXCEPTION OF:
PAGE 38: © KAREN FRANCIS
PAGE 180: © ISADORA JUKES
PAGE 218: © PETER FORRESTAL

PROOFREADING AND EDITING BY VICKY FISHER

PRINTED BY 1010 PRINTING INTERNATIONAL LIMITED, CHINA.

PUBLISHED BY GIANT DOG, A.B.N. 27 110 894 178. PO BOX 964, ROZELLE NSW 2039 AUSTRALIA
TELEPHONE: (+612) 9555 4077 FACSIMILE: (+612) 9555 5985
INFO@WINEDOGS.COM WEB: WWW.WINEDOGS.COM

FOR ORDERS: ORDERS@WINEDOGS.COM

OPINIONS EXPRESSED IN WINE DOGS ARE NOT NECESSARILY THOSE OF THE PUBLISHER.

ALL RIGHTS RESERVED. WITHOUT LIMITING THE RIGHTS UNDER COPYRIGHT RESERVED ABOVE, NO PART OF
THIS PUBLICATION MAY BE REPRODUCED, STORED IN OR INTRODUCED INTO A RETRIEVAL SYSTEM, OR TRANSMITTED,
IN ANY FORM OR BY ANY MEANS (ELECTRONIC, MECHANICAL, PHOTOCOPYING, RECORDING OR OTHERWISE),
WITHOUT THE PRIOR WRITTEN PERMISSION OF BOTH THE COPYRIGHT OWNER AND THE PUBLISHER OF THIS BOOK.

OTHER TITLES BY CRAIG McGILL AND SUSAN ELLIOTT INCLUDE:
WINE DOGS: ORIGINAL EDITION – THE DOGS OF AUSTRALIAN WINERIES ISBN 0-9580856-1-7
WINE DOGS: DELUXE EDITION – THE DOGS OF AUSTRALASIAN WINERIES ISBN 0-9580856-2-5
FOOTY DOGS: THE DOGS OF AUSTRALIAN RULES FOOTBALL ISBN 0-9580856-3-3
WINE DOGS AUSTRALIA – MORE DOGS FROM AUSTRALIAN WINERIES ISBN 978-1-921336-02-7
WINE DOGS AUSTRALIA 2 – MORE DOGS FROM AUSTRALIAN WINERIES ISBN 978-1-921336-16-4
WINE DOGS: USA EDITION – THE DOGS OF NORTH AMERICAN WINERIES ISBN 0-9580856-6-8
WINE DOGS USA 2 – MORE DOGS FROM NORTH AMERICAN WINERIES ISBN 978-1-921336-10-2
WINE DOGS USA 3 – MORE DOGS FROM NORTH AMERICAN WINERIES ISBN 978-1-921336-29-4
WINE DOGS ITALY – THE DOGS OF ITALIAN WINERIES ISBN 978-1-921336-11-9
WINE DOGS NEW ZEALAND – THE DOGS OF NEW ZEALAND WINERIES ISBN 978-1-921336-12-6

HEALTH WARNING: VETERINARY ASSOCIATIONS ADVISE THAT EATING GRAPES, SULTANAS OR RAISINS CAN MAKE A DOG EXTREMELY ILL AND COULD POSSIBLY RESULT IN FATAL KIDNEY FAILURE. IN THE INTERESTS OF CANINE HEALTH AND WELLBEING, DO NOT FEED YOUR DOG GRAPES OR ANY GRAPE BY-PRODUCT.

for Stella

CONTENTS

THE WILD BUNCH: A DOGGIE TALE ABOUT FRIENDSHIP, WISDOM AND THE PURSUIT OF THE PERFECT PINOT BY NICK RYAN	7
BARNABY — HOUND @ LARGE #19 BY NICK STOCK	41
WHY DOGS REALLY ARE THE BEST PEOPLE BY TORY SHEPHERD	71
THE TALE OF PINOT AND THE GREAT PORK BARRELLING SCANDAL OF 2010 BY EMMA MORONEY	89
A TALKING DOG BY ANDREW MARSH	113
EILEEN THE WIREHAIRED FOX TERRIER BY GREG DUNCAN POWELL	143
EDELWEISS ERNIE BY BEN CANAIDER	157
JOKER BY MATTHEW JUKES	179
A DOG OF A WINEMAKER BY TYSON STELZER	193
THE AUTOBIOGRAPHY OF FLING FORRESTAL BY PETER FORRESTAL	217
WHAT'S IN A NAME..? BY CRAIG McGILL	233
STATS, FACTS & WOOFILEAKS... BY CRAIG McGILL	234
WINERY AND VINEYARD LISTINGS	240
WINE DOGS BREED INDEX	251

XAN AND **JAZZ** SIX-YEAR-OLD KELPIE X'S, VOYAGER ESTATE, MARGARET RIVER WA

THE WILD BUNCH:
A DOGGIE TALE ABOUT FRIENDSHIP, WISDOM AND THE PURSUIT OF THE PERFECT PINOT

by Nick Ryan

IMAGINE THIS unlikely, unwelcome and frankly rather bizarre scenario.

A truckload of dogs, all shapes and sizes, all breeds, creeds and mis-deeds, rolls over somewhere in Central Australia.

Now before you get all up in arms, before you start bemoaning a great doggy tragedy, let me say no animals were harmed in the making of this far-fetched analogy.

So anyway, we're out here in the middle of this vast and unforgiving continent and we've got a motley collection of dogs by the side of the highway, all of them feeling a little dazed and confused.

Here's where instinct kicks in, that genetically hard-wired ability dogs have to get themselves from some far-flung spot to a place where their bowl is full, their blanket warm and their belly regularly rubbed.

The smartest dogs know that kind of poochie paradise can most likely be found in wine regions.

Dogs and winemakers go together like semillon and oysters, cabernet and roast lamb, Muscat and chocolate.

The fact you're holding the third edition of a book celebrating that uniquely deep bond is all the proof you need.

So our dogs dust themselves off, sniff the breeze and set out on their separate ways to find new homes in bucolic, vine-strewn landscapes.

The German Shepherd heads due south, down the Stuart Highway, towards the Barossa. The Doberman and the Rottweiler follow him, while a Dachshund waddles behind them in a vain attempt to catch up.

Somehow they just seem to know that this is where they belong, a place where they'll become part of families with names like Kalleske, Teusner, Scholz and Koch, where the scraps that fall from the dinner table will invariably be some form of smoked pig bits and they can roam freely among vineyards in places like Gnadenberg, St Jakobi and Hoffnungsthal.

The kelpies, blue heelers, cattle dogs and dingos head south west, following their noses until their nostrils pick up the briny tang of Margaret River's famous surf breaks.

Just as they are the distinctively Australian breeds, this is the distinctively Australian wine region, a landscape that could exist nowhere else other than this wafer of coast jutting out into the Indian Ocean.

This is where dogs can gorge on the scraps falling from hamburgers consumed with cabernet in beach-front carparks and revel in the fetid tang of roadkill wafting up to greet them as they stick their heads out of ute windows, barrelling through the ancient Karri forests.

The pampered, preened and handbag-housed stand by the roadside for hours, wondering why someone hasn't picked them up and smothered them with collagen kisses yet.

Eventually they realise they're going to have to save themselves. What better place for them then than Melbourne's so-called 'Dress Circle'.

Here they can sit on the poufs and chaises of Melbourne's old money estates on the Mornington Peninsula and in the Yarra Valley, or wander imperiously through the vine rows, safe in the knowledge that they're only an hour away from a decent doggycino in Toorak.

The pointers, retrievers and water dogs band together and start bounding in an easterly direction. They've heard tales of the unique tradition that takes hold in the Hunter Valley when the heavens open and the rain pours down.

As soon as the first drops hit that vineyard dirt the Hunter grapevine starts buzzing with the phrase "Good weather for ducks".

Unfortunately for the dogs, this isn't a hunting call or an ornithological observation.

It's actually a call for lunch.

With the weather making any real work almost impossible, all one Hunter winemaker has to do is utter the phrase and they'll all grab a bottle of great pinot noir and head off somewhere to eat their body weight in duck.

The dogs will be doubly disappointed when they learn that these tables don't shed scraps readily.

Finally the crash scene is deserted. The dogs are on their way.

They all have long arduous journeys ahead of them. The road before them is harsh and hard on the paws.

But when they reach their destinations, when they find their winemaking companions they can finally relax, content in the knowledge that doggy heaven is among the vines.

THROWN OUT OF UNIVERSITY IN ADELAIDE AND MOVING TO SYDNEY, **NICK RYAN** USED THE KNOWLEDGE HE'D GAINED RAIDING HIS OLD MAN'S CELLAR TO LAND A JOB WITH ONE OF SYDNEY'S LEADING WINE MERCHANTS. REALISING THAT WRITING ABOUT IT WAS EASIER THAN LIFTING IT HAS LED HIM TO WHERE HE IS NOW. HE'S A REGULAR CONTRIBUTOR TO *MEN'S STYLE AUSTRALIA*, *GOURMET TRAVELLER WINE*, *JAMES HALLIDAY'S WINE COMPANION MAGAZINE* AND WRITES A WEEKLY NEWSPAPER COLUMN IN ADELAIDE'S *SUNDAY MAIL* WHERE THE RUBBISH INSIDE HIS HEAD SPILLS OUT ONTO THE PAGE. HE IS PASSIONATE ABOUT WINES THAT ARE JUST AS INTERESTING BY THE FOURTH GLASS AS THEY ARE AT THE FIRST AND WOULD GIVE IT ALL UP TO PLAY ONE GAME FOR THE PORT ADELAIDE FOOTBALL CLUB.

BELLA

PET HATE: BATHS
OBSESSION: SLEEPING
OWNER: RANDEL BLACK
KNOWN ACCOMPLICE: BOO
FAVOURITE TOY: TENNIS BALLS
FAVOURITE PASTIME: CHASING STICKS
NAUGHTIEST DEED: EATING DRIPPER LINE

SARACEN ESTATES WILYABRUP, WA | STAFFORDSHIRE BULL TERRIER, 7

PET HATE: MAGPIES
OBSESSION: SLEEPING
OWNER: CARL BORRELLO
FAVOURITE FOOD: SARDINES
FAVOURITE TOY: STUFFED PIG
FAVOURITE PASTIME: SWIMMING
NAUGHTIEST DEED: CHASING KANGAROOS

MISSY

NEWFOUNDLAND, 4 | SARACEN ESTATES WILYABRUP, WA

JASPER

PET HATE: WATER
KNOWN ACCOMPLICE: SALLY
FAVOURITE TOY: TENNIS BALLS
OWNERS: THE SEPPELT FAMILY
NAUGHTIEST DEED: SPOOKING MICKEY THE CAT
FAVOURITE PASTIME: SLEEPING ON THE COUCH IN THE SUN
FAVOURITE FOOD: SNEAKY TREATS FROM TASTING ROOM VISITORS

MURRAY STREET VINEYARDS GREENOCK, SA | JACK RUSSELL TERRIER X, 1

FAVOURITE TOY: UTE TYRES
OWNERS: THE SEPPELT FAMILY
FAVOURITE PASTIME: HERDING THINGS
INCLUDING THE UTE AND HIS FAVOURITE TREE
FAVOURITE FOOD: THE JUICES FROM THE ROAST PAN
PET HATE: WATCHING THE UTE DRIVE AWAY WITHOUT HIM
NAUGHTIEST DEED: BARKING WHILE ON THE BACK OF THE UTE

COOPER

HUNTAWAY X 8 | **MURRAY STREET VINEYARDS** GREENOCK, SA

JAGO

FAVOURITE TOY: TENNIS BALL
OWNERS: BRUCE AND DIANA KEIR
OBSESSION: WATCHING AND WAITING FOR MICE
NAUGHTIEST DEED: BEING LED ASTRAY BY DIESEL
PET HATE: BEING TOLD HE CAN'T COME TO A PARTY
KNOWN ACCOMPLICE: JUDY GARLAND THE BULL TERRIER
FAVOURITE FOOD: LOCAL SOUTH ROCK SMOKED LAMB ON THE BONE
FAVOURITE PASTIME: GREETING CUSTOMERS WITH AN IMPORTANT BARK

CHAPMAN RIVER WINES KANGAROO ISLAND, SA | JACK RUSSELL TERRIER, 7

PET HATE: WATER
FAVOURITE FOOD: CHEESE
OWNERS: CHRIS AND JILL MILNER
FAVOURITE PASTIME: CHASING BUTTERFLIES
NAUGHTIEST DEED: KILLING BABY BLACKBIRDS
OBSESSION: CHASING STRAY DOGS OFF THE PROPERTY
KNOWN ACCOMPLICE: JOEY THE TENTERFIELD TERRIER

JESSIE

POPPY

PET HATE: THE HAIR DRYER
OWNERS: ALISTER AND ROSA PURBRICK
FAVOURITE FOOD: BEEF BRISKET BONES
NAUGHTIEST DEEDS: DESTROYING THONGS AND CHEWING ON THE OUTDOOR FURNITURE
FAVOURITE TOY: ANYTHING SHE CAN PULL APART
FAVOURITE PASTIMES: PLAYING WITH TESS AND HUNTING RABBITS

TAHBILK WINES TABILK, VIC | LABRADOODLE. 1

OWNER: HAYLEY PURBRICK
PET HATE: POPPY STEALING THE SHOW
OBSESSION: CHASING RABBITS WITH POPPY
FAVOURITE TOY: HAYLEY'S OLD STUFFED DOG
NAUGHTIEST DEED: TEARING UP HER BABYSITTER'S CHAIRS
FAVOURITE PASTIME: 'DIVE AND TACKLE' WITH HER BEST MATE POPPY

TESS

KELPIE X, 1 | **TAHBILK WINERY** TABILK, VIC

SHEEBA

OBSESSION: TENNIS BALLS
PET HATE: VACUUM CLEANERS
OWNERS: THE GHUMMAN FAMILY
NAUGHTIEST DEED: DEMOLISHING A LAMB CURRY DINNER FOR SIX PEOPLE
FAVOURITE FOODS: APPLES FROM THE TREES
FAVOURITE PASTIME: CHASING BIRDS OUT OF THE NETS

NAZAARAY ESTATE WINERY FLINDERS, VIC | LABRADOR, 8

TASH

OWNERS: ANDREW AND SAMANTHA FERRELL
FAVOURITE FOOD: HOMEMADE DOG RISOTTO
OBSESSION: STEALING WINE BARREL BUNGS
FAVOURITE PASTIME: TUG-OF-WAR WITH BRUNO
FAVOURITE TOY: ANYTHING SHE CAN RIP THE STUFFING OUT OF
NAUGHTIEST DEED: TRAILING DIRTY PAW PRINTS THROUGH THE CELLAR DOOR

EDEN ROAD WINES MURRUMBATEMAN, NSW | BULL ARAB X, 2

TINKER

PET HATE: BEING WASHED
FAVOURITE FOOD: CHICKEN NECKS
NAUGHTIEST DEED: DISAPPEARING
OBSESSION: BIRDS ON THE GROUND
OWNERS: ANNETTE AND DOUG BALNAVES
FAVOURITE PASTIMES: SLEEPING AND HUNTING
KNOWN ACCOMPLICES: PETER, KIRSTY AND THE GRANDCHILDREN

BALNAVES OF COONAWARRA COONAWARRA, SA | JACK RUSSELL TERRIER, 4

OWNER: NICK BROWN
FAVOURITE TOY: FOOTBALL
FAVOURITE PASTIME: CHASING BIRDS
PET HATE: LEO, THE ST LEONARDS CAT
FAVOURITE FOOD: DRIED KANGAROO TAILS
NAUGHTIEST DEED: CHASING THE CHICKENS
OBSESSION: NEVER MISSING A RIDE IN THE BACK OF THE UTE

MOLLY

BORDER COLLIE, 1 | ALL SAINTS ESTATE WAHGUNYAH, VIC

MAX

FAVOURITE PASTIME: BEING THE WORLD'S FASTEST COUCH POTATO
PET HATE: THE SMELL OF HIS OWN GAS
NAUGHTIEST DEEDS: STEALING GUESTS' PICNICS AND CLEARING THE ROOM WITH GAS
OBSESSION: CATCHING THE VACUUM CLEANER
OWNERS: CRAIG AND JENNIFER BRENT-WHITE
FAVOURITE FOOD: A GOOD BBQ FOLLOWED BY ICE CREAM

MONTY

NAUGHTIEST DEED: HUMPING
FAVOURITE PASTIME: LICKING SPILT WINE FROM BARREL TOPPING
FAVOURITE FOOD: BLUE SWIMMER CRABS AND DHUFISH LIGHTLY GRILLED
OWNERS: CRAIG AND JENNIFER BRENT-WHITE
OBSESSION: HUMPING MAX AT EVERY OPPORTUNITY
PET HATE: NOT GETTING HER TEN HOURS BEAUTY SLEEP

CAPE NATURALISTE VINEYARD YALLINGUP, WA | OLD ENGLISH SHEEPDOG X, 3 & JACK RUSSELL TERRIER, 6

DAISY
PET HATE: THINGS NOT HAPPENING QUICKLY ENOUGH
OWNERS: THE BURGE FAMILY
FAVOURITE PASTIME: MEETING PEOPLE
KNOWN ACCOMPLICES: JESSIE AND LIBBI
FAVOURITE TOY: ANYTHING JESSIE HAS
OBSESSION: BEING FIRST AT EVERYTHING

JESSIE
FAVOURITE FOOD: APPLES FROM THE TREE
FAVOURITE TOY: DAISY
FAVOURITE PASTIME: CUDDLING ON THE COUCH
OWNERS: THE BURGE FAMILY
PET HATE: NUM-NUM THE CORELLA
OBSESSION: DISCIPLINING THE CORELLA

DUDLEY
PET HATE: BATHS
FAVOURITE TOY: SOFT TOY CALLED DEREK
OWNERS: THE BURGE FAMILY
KNOWN ACCOMPLICES: ANYONE NOT TOO BOISTEROUS
OBSESSION: HOOVERING THE KITCHEN FLOOR EVERY MORNING
FAVOURITE FOOD: FRESH BONES

LOFTY

PET HATE: AN EMPTY DINNER BOWL
FAVOURITE TOYS: DESTUFFED BUNNY AND MANCHESTER UNITED SOCCER BALL
NAUGHTIEST DEED: EATING $5.00 NOTES
OBSESSIONS: TOILET ROLLS AND SWIMMING
FAVOURITE PASTIME: CHASING LITTLE LIZARDS
OWNERS: SHARON PEARSON AND GARRY SWEENEY

MT LOFTY RANGES LENSWOOD, SA | LABRADOR, 6 MONTHS

FAVOURITE TOY: BLUE CROCHETED BLANKET
OBSESSIONS: BABY MAX AND BELLY TICKLES
OWNERS: GREG COOLEY AND KELLI SHANAHAN
FAVOURITE FOOD: ANYTHING ANYONE ELSE HAS
KNOWN ACCOMPLICES: JACK, RUBY AND PHOEBE
NAUGHTIEST DEED: SHREDDING A LOUNGE CHAIR
PET HATE: BEING SEPARATED FROM GREG AND MAX
FAVOURITE PASTIME: GREETING/SNOUTING CUSTOMERS

MICKEY

GREYHOUND, 6 | GREG COOLEY WINES CLARE, SA

OWNER: MARTIN PFEIFFER
FAVOURITE TOY: MOTORBIKE WHEELS
NAUGHTIEST DEED: IGNORING DR HARRY AND THE TV CREW TO CHASE A RABBIT
PET HATE: SHARING FOOD WITH WALLY THE CAT
KNOWN ACCOMPLICE: BUTTONS THE KANGAROO
OBSESSION: BEING WINGMAN IN THE WHISTLER TRUCK
FAVOURITE PASTIME: PERFORMING ON TV WITH DR HARRY

MARLO

FAVOURITE FOOD: SARDINES
PET HATE: HAVING TO STAND UP TO EAT
OWNERS: KRISTEN PRYCE AND TOM WILKS
FAVOURITE TOY: HALF-CHEWED TOY CAMEL
OBSESSION: SMUGGLING HIS TOYS IN AND OUT OF THE HOUSE
NAUGHTIEST DEED: JUMPING ON WHITE QUILT COVERS WITH DIRTY PAWS
FAVOURITE PASTIMES: SWIMMING AT THE BEACH OR GETTING A BELLY RUB

WANGOLINA STATION MOUNT BENSON, SA | AUSTRALIAN SHEPHERD, 2

FAVOURITE PASTIME: SNORING
OWNERS: MARTINE AND PAUL CARPENTER
PET HATES: WATER HOSES AND OTHER DOGS
FAVOURITE TOYS: BUNGS AND TENNIS BALLS
OBSESSION: THE PAMPERED POOCH'S MANICURES
NAUGHTIEST DEED: IN HER YOUNGER DAYS,
REGULARLY MAKING DEPOSITS IN THE CFO'S OFFICE
KNOWN ACCOMPLICES: ANYONE WILLING TO THROW A BALL HER WAY

ZOE

LABRADOR, 9 | *WIRRA WIRRA VINEYARDS* McLAREN VALE, SA

WEBBER

OWNER: MARK BULMAN
PET HATE: HOT AIR BALLOONS
FAVOURITE FOOD: AGED BONES
OBSESSIONS: BALLS AND STICKS
FAVOURITE TOYS: BALLS AND STICKS
KNOWN ACCOMPLICES: NEIL, PAULINE AND HEATHER
FAVOURITE PASTIME: HANGING OUT WITH THE VINEYARD TEAM

TURKEY FLAT VINEYARDS TANUNDA, SA | KELPIE X, 1

PET HATE: POSSUMS
FAVOURITE FOOD: SCHMACKOS
FAVOURITE PASTIME: SLEEPING
FAVOURITE TOY: STUFFED LION CUB
OWNERS: MICHAEL AND WENDY O'DEA
NAUGHTIEST DEED: SCRATCHING UP THE CARPET TRYING TO CATCH A MOUSE
OBSESSION: GETTING ATTENTION AND PATS
KNOWN ACCOMPLICES: BONNIE AND CLYDE

MOLLY

SHIH TZU X, 2 | DIONYSUS WINERY MURRUMBATEMAN, NSW

CHARLIE BROWN
PET HATE: ANGRY PEOPLE
OWNERS: WARREN AND NICKY RANDALL
NAUGHTIEST DEED: HUNTING NATIVE FEASTS
FAVOURITE FOODS: ROAST CHICKEN AND MEDIUM RARE FILLET STEAK
FAVOURITE PASTIME: BEING PHOTOGRAPHED WITH CELLAR DOOR CUSTOMERS
OBSESSIONS: POINTING AND CHASING RABBITS AT SEPPELTSFIELD

LUCY
NAUGHTIEST DEED: CHEWING THE CORNERS OFF A SHEEPSKIN RUG
FAVOURITE TOY: LITTLE BLUE MONKEY
OWNERS: WARREN AND NICKY RANDALL
PET HATE: THE EXHAUST NOTE OF THE FERRARI
FAVOURITE FOODS: SALMON SASHIMI AND PISTACHIOS
OBSESSION: HUNTING RATS AROUND THE CHICKEN COOP

OWNER: ANDREW NUGENT
KNOWN ACCOMPLICE: BANDIT
PET HATES: RABBITS AND PLANES
FAVOURITE TOY: LARGE TEDDY BEAR
OBSESSIONS: RABBITS AND CHASING PLANES
NAUGHTIEST DEED: TAKING A CUPCAKE OFF A WEDDING CAKE
FAVOURITE PASTIME: WAITING FOR FOOD FROM WINERY STAFF

HORATIO

BORDER COLLIE, 3 | **BIRD IN HAND** WOODSIDE, SA

GRACIE

OWNER: DAVE POWELL
PET HATE: LITTLE PEOPLE
FAVOURITE FOOD: CHICKEN NECKS
NAUGHTIEST DEED: DESTROYING A DOONA
KNOWN ACCOMPLICES: SHADOW AND COCOA
OBSESSIONS: CHASING ANYTHING THAT MOVES
FAVOURITE PASTIME: GOING FOR A DRIVE IN THE CAR

TORBRECK VINTNERS MARANANGA, SA | KELPIE, 3

FAVOURITE TOY: A GIANT PINK FLEA
OWNERS: BRETT AND KERRY HOUSE
KNOWN ACCOMPLICE: ELVIS THE PUG
OBSESSIONS: BAXTER THE CAT AND FOOD
PET HATE: BEING LEFT AT HOME DURING VINTAGE
NAUGHTIEST DEED: NIPPING PEOPLE'S FEET TO GET ATTENTION

KACEE

BARNABY – HOUND @ LARGE

by Nick Stock

MERMAIDS! AWESOME! Wait, I'm underwater, I can't swim, no, no way, how did, what am I going to...

Whoooooaaa, dreaming. Ok just act cool and lay still. Hmm doesn't sound like anyone's home so no chance I've been entertaining the masses with my sleep twitches, yelps and grunts. Apparently it's the funniest thing going and especially hysterical after dinner. Nothing quite like waking up to half a dozen people pointing at you and laughing. Humans do plenty of dumb stuff but you don't see dogs rolling around in fits of laughter. Seriously rude behaviour that. If they didn't feed us they'd be dead set useless.

Not that I'm going to whinge. I mean, it's summer, we're at the beach and I'm getting properly fed around the clock on human food. Yep, you name it and I'm eating it. This hot weather gets the dreams going though, never thought I'd come face to face with a mermaid. Come to think of it, the holiday diet could also be firing the dreams along.

Had a big barbeque over here in McLaren Vale last night, plenty of the mega marbled dry-aged Coorong Black Angus made its way down to me at ground level too. Don't think I ought to get too used to it, which is probably a good thing. I'll end up as fat as Doug, maybe fatter. I wonder if that's possible.

I'm a flavour chaser as much as the next pooch, and very discerning when it comes to meats I might add, but I just can't believe how they get all the texture in that Coorong Black Angus as well as so much flavour. Oops, drooling now; lucky I'm on the rug.

No chance I'll ever get to do it but Doug and Denise went to this grain-fed vs. grass-fed beef extravaganza the other week and they couldn't stop talking about it. Man, it sounded awesome.

Dougie's a flat out grass-fed lover, it's all about the flavour for him, whereas Denise is all about that luxurious marbled texture. She loves a bit of luxury our Denise and who can blame her. She keeps the Champagne houses busy, man can she put the fizz away!

Doug's been on a solid beer during the day and big walloping reds at night since we arrived here at the beach. Plenty of the old Penfolds Bin 389 stacked up for Tuesday's recycling, let me tell ya. Must be the perfect wine for all those tasty grill flavours, wonder what it tastes like? I reckon I'd like it.

That Peter Gago seems like a nice bloke too. Doug took me for a walk up to Magill Estate a couple of years back and we ran into him. There I was getting a pat from none other than the Penfolds Chief Winemaker. How good is that!

Now here's a funny thing, Doug was telling Denise he wants to try his hand at winemaking the other night. I was under the table pretending to sleep after they'd had dinner and Doug had a couple of reds under the belt when he dropped the "I think I want to be a winemaker" bombshell. I lost control of my bum at that point and dropped a bombshell of my own for which I copped a love tap from the sandshoe.

The funniest part was Denise managed to keep her cool and egged him on for a good 15 minutes before Doug realised she was taking the piss. She's pretty much got him figured out – reads him like a book. Loves him dearly too, I might add.

Anyhow, after I stopped laughing and farting I started thinking about what life on the vineyard might be like. Fair dinkum, I reckon it's for me. Imagine working the crowd at cellar door on the weekends, how good would that be? Lounging around on the picnic blankets under a big tree and being fed like a king.

I reckon those wine dogs all look perfectly happy and why wouldn't they be? Plenty of open space would be a bonus, not that I'm huge on the exercise, but the view from the winery deck would have to be pretty bloody good. Très relaxing.

That's what I'd do, more a supervisor's kind of role, looking out over the vines, that's more my speed. Wonder what vintage would be like? I bet the smell of grapes fermenting is awesome. Maybe I could get into a bit of winemaking; I mean, it's mostly just standing around watching other people do stuff apparently.

Can't be that hard and I reckon Doug would be the happiest man on the planet. He'd love it. I wonder how serious he was being or if it was just the wine talking? He'd want a restaurant too I reckon. That'd be good. Geez, I've gotta get this over the line.

Imagine having your own winery. I might even get on the label or, better still, they might even name a wine after me. Now that would be something. Damn, I might even get my ugly mug in that Wine Dogs *book – how cool would that be!*

NICK STOCK IS ONE OF AUSTRALIA'S MOST PROLIFIC WINE COMMENTATORS WHOSE INVOLVEMENT IN WINE STRETCHES WELL BEYOND WRITING TO RADIO AND TELEVISION BROADCASTING, WINE SHOW JUDGING, PUBLIC SPEAKING, EDUCATING AND WINEMAKING. HIS DOGGED PURSUIT OF GREAT WINE TAKES HIM ALL OVER THE PLACE AND HE'S COME TO RECOGNISE THAT WHEREVER GREAT WINE IS MADE, THERE'S USUALLY A GREAT DOG NEARBY. WWW.WINELENS.COM.AU (YOU CAN READ MORE ABOUT BARNABY'S ADVENTURES IN *WINE DOGS AUSTRALIA* AND *WINE DOGS AUSTRALIA 2.*)

PET HATE: BEING ALONE
OWNER: LACHLAN MILHINCH
FAVOURITE FOOD: BACON RIND
FAVOURITE PASTIME: PLAYING FETCH
FAVOURITE TOY: SQUEAKY MR OINKER
NAUGHTIEST DEED: EATING THE CHOOKS
OBSESSION: BIRD CONTROL UNDER VINEYARD NETS

MR BUSTER

RHODESIAN RIDGEBACK X, 2 | *SCION VINEYARD & WINERY* RUTHERGLEN, VIC

LUCCA

FAVOURITE FOOD: MANKY BONES
OBSESSIONS: STALKING GRASSHOPPERS AND FISHING IN ROCKPOOLS AT THE BEACH
OWNERS: SIMON AND FRANCESCA STEELE
PET HATES: FROSTY MORNINGS AND HOME RENOVATIONS
NAUGHTIEST DEED: THE "HOUDINI INCIDENT" INVOLVING SALLY HARROP AND ENDANGERED BLUE-BILLED WATERFOWL
FAVOURITE PASTIME: CLIMBING UNDER DOONAS FOR A SNOOZE
KNOWN ACCOMPLICES: GERTIE AND AMADEUS THE DANCING JACK RUSSELL

BROKENWOOD WINES POKOLBIN, NSW | HUNGARIAN VIZSLA, 4

OBSESSION: WOMEN
FAVOURITE TOY: DUCKY
OWNER: NATHAN HUGHES
KNOWN ACCOMPLICE: MELISSA LEE
FAVOURITE PASTIME: BEATING UP HAMISH
FAVOURITE FOOD: ANYTHING BUT PRAWNS
NAUGHTIEST DEED: RUNNING OFF TO THE LOCAL
LAKE TO SKINNY DIP WITH HIS NEWFOUND LADY

THOMAS

BOXER X, 6 MONTHS | **BROKENWOOD WINES** POKOLBIN, NSW

SPIKE

OWNER: SARAH GUTHRIE
FAVOURITE TOY: DEAD RATS
FAVOURITE PASTIME: RATTING
OBSESSION: DIGGING FOR RATS
NAUGHTIEST DEED: PRETENDING TO BE A SHEEP DOG
KNOWN ACCOMPLICES: SELWOOD, SCARLETT, TED AND BART
PET HATE: BEING TIED UP AND NOT BEING ABLE TO LOOK FOR RATS

GRAMPIANS ESTATE GREAT WESTERN, VIC | JACK RUSSELL TERRIER X, 5

SCARLETT

FAVOURITE TOY: THE HOUSE CAT
OWNERS: TOM AND SARAH GUTHRIE
OBSESSION: SUPPORTING GEELONG
PET HATE: COLLINGWOOD SUPPORTERS
NAUGHTIEST DEED: CHASING THE HORSES
KNOWN ACCOMPLICES: THE OTHER DOGS;
BROWNLESS, COUCHIE, BART AND TED

SELWOOD

FAVOURITE TOY: THE SHERRIN
OWNERS: TOM AND SARAH GUTHRIE
PET HATE: AFL VIDEO REVIEW SYSTEM
NAUGHTIEST DEED: HOLDING THE BALL
FAVOURITE FOOD: FOUR 'N TWENTY MEAT PIE
FAVOURITE PASTIME: WATCHING 2011 GRAND FINAL REPLAYS

BORDER COLLIE, 4 & KELPIE, 2   **GRAMPIANS ESTATE** GREAT WESTERN, VIC

FEATHERTOP

OWNERS: KEL AND JANELLE BOYNTON
OBSESSION: CHEWING HIS OWN FOOT
PET HATES: DELIVERY TRUCKS AND UTES
FAVOURITE FOOD: NANNY KIM'S ROAST DINNERS
NAUGHTIEST DEED: SNEAKING INTO CELLAR DOOR
FAVOURITE PASTIME: JUMPING ON PEOPLE'S LAPS AND LOOKING CUTE
KNOWN ACCOMPLICES: ZAC THE DOG, CHILLI AND CHARLOTTE THE FARM PIG

BOYNTON'S FEATHERTOP WINERY POREPUNKAH, VIC | MALTESE X, 7

OWNER: BEN PORTET
OBSESSION: POSSUMS
FAVOURITE FOOD: BOMBE ALASKA
PET HATE: SMALL WHITE FLUFFY DOGS
FAVOURITE TOYS: BUNGS AND RED KONG BALL
KNOWN ACCOMPLICES: BOB THE HALF DOG AND POPPY
FAVOURITE PASTIME: BOTHERING SMALL WHITE FLUFFY DOGS

BOMBE ALASKA

GERMAN SHORTHAIRED POINTER, 2 | **DOMINIQUE PORTET** COLDSTREAM, VIC

SCOOBY

OWNER: CAROLYN STEVENS
PET HATE: THE WINE AGITATOR
FAVOURITE TOY: SQUEAKY GUM BOOT TOY
KNOWN ACCOMPLICE: HENRY THE DONKEY
FAVOURITE PASTIME: SLEEPING IN CAROLYN'S CHAIR AFTER RUNNING THROUGH A MUDDY VINEYARD
OBSESSION: TOUCHING NOSES WITH HENRY THE DONKEY
NAUGHTIEST DEED: STEALING SOCKS FROM UNATTENDED GUM BOOTS

GRAHAM STEVENS WINES McLAREN FLAT, SA | MINIATURE GROODLE, 3

MEL
FAVOURITE TOY: MAX
OWNER: JIM LUMBERS
PET HATE: VACUUM CLEANER
FAVOURITE PASTIME: SLEEPING
OBSESSION: THE VACUUM CLEANER
NAUGHTIEST DEED: HAVING 15 PUPPIES

MAX
OBSESSION: RABBITS
OWNER: JIM LUMBERS
FAVOURITE FOOD: CHICKEN NECKS
FAVOURITE PASTIME: HARASSING MEL
PET HATE: NOT BEING ALLOWED TO SIT ON JIM'S LAP
NAUGHTIEST DEED: EATING A GOSLING FROM THE NEST ON THE DAM

JACK RUSSELL TERRIER, 11 & ITALIAN GREYHOUND X, 1 | LERIDA ESTATE LAKE GEORGE, NSW

CHARLIE BROWN

OBSESSION: FRISBEES
OWNER: VIRGINIA JACOBS
FAVOURITE FOOD: ALMONDS
NAUGHTIEST DEED: TEARING HOLES IN STUFFED TOYS – CURRENT RECORD 1.5 MINUTES
FAVOURITE TOY: ANY STUFFED TOY WITH A SQUEAKER
KNOWN ACCOMPLICES: ROSIE, RUBY, LEILA AND FOODLE
FAVOURITE PASTIME: SITTING IN FRONT OF THE FIRE IN WINTER

MITCHELTON WINES NAGAMBIE, VIC | POODLE, 8

PET HATE: BEING LEFT AT HOME
OWNERS: ELIZA, DENIS AND COCO
KNOWN ACCOMPLICES: LEO THE CAT AND MOLLY
FAVOURITE PASTIME: TRYING TO CATCH LEO THE CAT
OBSESSION: ANYTHING SMALLER AND FURRIER THAN HIM
NAUGHTIEST DEED: EATING THE ELECTRICAL CORD FOR THE GATE
FAVOURITE TOY: STUFFED BLUE HEELER DOG GIVEN TO HIM BY COCO

HUGO

GERMAN SHEPHERD, 7 MONTHS | ST LEONARDS VINEYARD WAHGUNYAH, VIC

ADY
OWNER: KEITH BARNES
PET HATE: SMALL PEOPLE
KNOWN ACCOMPLICE: LU LU
OBSESSION: FOOD OF ALL KIND
FAVOURITE PASTIME: SWIMMING AFTER THE DUCKS
NAUGHTIEST DEED: GETTING STUCK DOWN A RABBIT HOLE

LU LU
OWNER: KEITH BARNES
FAVOURITE FOOD: LAMB
KNOWN ACCOMPLICE: ADY
FAVOURITE TOY: TENNIS SET
FAVOURITE PASTIME: RIDING ON THE ATV
NAUGHTIEST DEED: BEING AN ESCAPE ARTIST

OWNER: ROBERT BLACK
KNOWN ACCOMPLICE: RAY
FAVOURITE FOOD: EGG AND BACON ROLLS
PET HATES: NEW YEAR'S EVE AND THE VET
OBSESSION: PLAYING FRISBEE IN THE DAM
FAVOURITE PASTIME: DELIVERING WINE IN THE VAN
NAUGHTIEST DEED: CHEWING A USB STICK INTO PIECES

MARTY

LABRADOR X, 2 | **BUNNAMAGOO WINES** *MUDGEE, NSW*

REMUS

PET HATE: THUNDER
OWNER: ALEXANDRA BAIRD
FAVOURITE PASTIMES: CHASING RABBITS AND ROLLING IN KANGAROO DROPPINGS
FAVOURITE FOOD: STEAK AND LIVER TREATS
NAUGHTIEST DEED: DESTROYING DESIGNER SHOES
FAVOURITE TOY: STUFFED TEDDY BEAR (NOW RESEMBLES ROADKILL)
OBSESSION: CHASING HIS TENNIS BALL THEN DIVING INTO THE DAM

GENESIS VINEYARD AND FARMHOUSE ROTHBURY, NSW | KELPIE X, 4

OWNER: COL DALEY
PET HATE: TRACTORS
FAVOURITE TOY: ANY BALL
FAVOURITE PASTIME: CHASING BIRDS
OBSESSION: TRYING TO BITE TRACTOR TYRES
NAUGHTIEST DEED: REFUSING TO JUMP UP INTO THE UTE
KNOWN ACCOMPLICES: COL, WAGS, SAM, GUS AND LUCKY

BRIGHTY

CATTLE DOG, 3 | *ELING FOREST WINERY* SUTTON FOREST, NSW

AXLE
FAVOURITE TOY: MAJOR
FAVOURITE FOOD: LAYING HENS
OBSESSION: NOISES IN THE NIGHT
OWNERS: CHARLIE AND VIRGINIA MELTON
FAVOURITE PASTIME: SITTING OUTSIDE KFC
KNOWN ACCOMPLICES: MAJOR AND CHARLIE

MAJOR
FAVOURITE TOY: CATS
PET HATE: MUSICALS ABOUT CATS
OBSESSION: CATS (NOT THE MUSICAL)
FAVOURITE PASTIME: LOOKING FOR CATS
OWNERS: CHARLIE AND VIRGINIA MELTON
KNOWN ACCOMPLICES: NOT ANDREW LLOYD WEBBER

DALMATIANS, 7 | **CHARLES MELTON WINES** TANUNDA, SA

CYDI

OWNER: JACOB STEIN
FAVOURITE TOY: SOCCER BALL
OBSESSION: ATTACKING BUNGS
FAVOURITE FOOD: KANGAROO MINCE
KNOWN ACCOMPLICES: COOPER, TRUFFLE AND PEPPER
FAVOURITE PASTIME: RUNNING BESIDE THE MOTORBIKE
NAUGHTIEST DEED: TAKING THE BUNGS OUT OF FERMENTING BARRELS

ROBERT STEIN WINERY MUDGEE, NSW | KELPIE, 2

WHY DOGS REALLY ARE
THE BEST PEOPLE

by Tory Shepherd

DON'T GET ME WRONG; I REALLY LIKE HUMANS. Some of my best friends are humans. Humans can do all sorts of amazing things. They built the Large Hadron Collider so they can smash particles into each other and learn more about the Big Bang, and they invented Hypercolour t-shirts and Spam. They invented long lunches and cheese and can turn grape juice into wine.

But dogs are better. Here's why.

THEY DON'T JUDGE

Humans are very judgemental creatures. Helmet-haired ladies in department stores judge you with a sniffy up and down look. Especially if you're wearing ugg boots.

Pubs and clubs judge you if you're tattooed or semi-clad. Or, again, wearing ugg boots.

We judge each other daily on our clothes and our hairstyles, our religions, our skin colour. Pick almost any human characteristic and you can be sure there's another human who'll judge you on it. Flabby skin under your arms? Judged. Red hair? Judged. Monobrow? Judged.

Dogs don't care. They'll pretty much hang out with anyone. Other dogs, of course. Goofy little mutts with overbites or trussed up poodles with topiary hair, it's all the same to them. Down in the doggie park they don't even notice if another dog's got Swarovski crystals embedded in its collar or mange on its backside.

This counts for humans as well; tall, short, fat, thin. Dogs don't care. Scientologists, hippies, nerds. The Mormons may cop it a bit, but that's just because of their door-knocking schtick.

Unlike pretty much everyone else I know, my dog has never been too embarrassed to walk down the street with me. And he really likes my ugg boots.

THEY'RE GOOD LISTENERS

Being able to listen to others is a rare skill these days. Most people want to interject with their own stories, or – worse – interject some horrid, florid bit of pop psychology or throw in a quote from Deepak Chopra.

Next time you're lurking about with your mates at the pub, watch how people fail to listen. They hover, lean forward as though they're paying attention, but really they're just waiting for your next breath so they can jump in with a story about how the exact same thing happened to them only better/ worse/ louder/ with a better-looking chick.

It's the same in business meetings. The guy from marketing sitting there with his fingers pensively intertwined isn't deeply pondering your great idea; he's working out how to gazump you in front of the new boss.

So no-one listens. But (oh!) how we love to be listened to. And this is where dogs are wonderful. They just absorb, and look at you as though you're revealing deep insights about the ways of the world. I was talking my dog through a recipe for peanut butter ice-cream the other day (buy ice-cream, add peanut butter) and he looked at me as though I was George Calombariss.

The best of them cock their heads slightly, perk their ears up just so, give a wag of the tail, and settle in comfortably for the long haul. And if it gets emotional they might just warmly lean against you, or give you a comforting lick. And sometimes, that's all we really need, isn't it?

THEY DON'T START WARS

And it's not because they're not territorial. They really are.

But they lack the nastiness of humans that makes them wage sustained battles against each other. They lack lust for power. They lack greed (except for food). Frankly, they lack the attention span and the organisational ability. One sniff of a rabbit and they'd completely lose track of the people they're trying to decimate.

If dogs ruled the world, there would be peace on Earth. And I, for one, would welcome our canine overlords.

THEY'RE SIMPLE

God bless humans. They put a lot of effort into things. But that also means they often make life too damn complicated. No-one has a plain old barbie these days. It's gotta be marinated saltbush lamb or Angus beef with fennel and blood orange salad. And a cider tasting.

Kids' birthday parties are no longer just honeyjoys and chocolate crackles; they need to be gluten-free, preservative-free, organic free-range extravaganzas with some spectacularly perfect cake that actually looks like the pictures in the Australian Women's Weekly Birthday Cake Book.

Dogs are simple. They like anything, as long as it's vaguely meaty. Sometimes they don't even need that. They don't need their eggs truffled, or their water sparkling. They don't need gadgets or tablets or cup holders in cars. They're simple, so they're happy. There's a lesson in that. I'm just going to install the Wikipedia app so I can work out what it is and then I'll sync the answer to my iCloud.

UNCONDITIONAL LOVE

The number one reason dogs are better than people is that they love you unconditionally.

You can chuck a tantrum and call them names and they'll just drop their ears and look at you adoringly. They don't mind your snoring or your morning breath. They don't care if you never went to university and they don't care if you don't shut your mouth when you chew. They just love you anyway.

Human relationships are complex minefields, full of constant compromises, and often we behave the worst with the people we love the most. Familiarity breeds contempt.

Not with dogs. They have boundless affection for their pack. From the smallest child who pats them repetitively on the nose (when they'd really like their ears scratched) to the oldest member of the family who keeps wanting to send them outside (but makes up for it by accidentally dropping food on the floor), dogs love their families unconditionally.

That's why dogs really are the best people.

It's true oooh-oooh that he loves me more than you
I'm down, bring him round, let him jump up on me now
Okay so he thinks he's a human sometimes
I forget everything when I look into his eyes
It's true dogs are the best people
His love comes free and unconditionally.

– **THE FAUVES**, *DOGS ARE THE BEST PEOPLE (1996)*

TORY SHEPHERD IS AN AWARD-WINNING JOURNALIST AND COLUMNIST WITH *THE ADVERTISER* AND *THE PUNCH*. SHE LIVES AMONG THE VINES IN THE GLORIOUS ADELAIDE HILLS WITH HER BORDER COLLIE SANGIO (PICTURED ABOVE) AND WINEMAKER/VITICULTURALIST HUSBAND DAMIEN, AND CAN OFTEN BE SEEN WALKING AROUND THE AREA IN AN ATTEMPT TO STAVE OFF WINE-PAUNCH. SHE IS, HOWEVER, EASILY DISTRACTED FROM THESE HEALTHY PURSUITS BY THE OFFER OF WINE, SO IF YOU SHOULD SEE HER PASS BY...

PASCOE

PET HATE: BATH TIME
OWNER: JUSTIN McNAMEE
OBSESSION: STEALING JUSTIN'S CLOTHES
FAVOURITE FOOD: ANYTHING AND EVERYTHING AND LOTS OF IT
FAVOURITE PASTIME: DINING AT CHAPEL HILL GOURMET RETREAT
NAUGHTIEST DEED: VISITING OTHER CELLAR DOORS TO CHECK OUT THEIR FOOD SUPPLIES

SAMUEL'S GORGE MCLAREN VALE, SA | LONG-HAIRED WEIMARANER, 8

FAVOURITE TOY: BUNGS
OWNER: AARON HANCOCK
FAVOURITE FOOD: PEANUT BUTTER ON TOAST
KNOWN ACCOMPLICES: COCO, ROSIE AND DAISY
PET HATES: BEING BRUSHED AND LAWN MOWERS
OBSESSIONS: EATING AND CAR RIDES WITH HIS FOLKS
NAUGHTIEST DEED: EATING A ROAST CHICKEN FROM OFF THE BENCH

BLAISE

SIBERIAN HUSKY, 8 | **COLDSTREAM HILLS** COLDSTREAM, VIC

LUCY

OWNER: JAN SIEMELINK-ALLEN
FAVOURITE FOOD: MARROW BONES
FAVOURITE PASTIME: RUNNING WITH THE MOTORBIKE THROUGH THE VINEYARD
FAVOURITE TOY: HER SHEEPSKIN RUGGY
PET HATE: OTHER DOGS TAKING HER SPACE
KNOWN ACCOMPLICES: SAVVY, BENTLY AND DIBBA
NAUGHTIEST DEED: HIDING BONES INSIDE THE CAR

BARRISTERS BLOCK WINES WOODSIDE, SA | LABRADOR, 5

FAVOURITE FOOD: PIGS EARS
FAVOURITE TOY: ANYTHING THAT SQUEAKS
OBSESSION: RUNNING AS FAST AS A CHEETAH
OWNERS: JACKIE BARTON AND ADRIAN JONES
FAVOURITE PASTIME: CHASING STICKS IN THE YARD
PET HATE: BEING MISTAKEN FOR A TASMANIAN TIGER
NAUGHTIEST DEED: PINCHING THE ROASTING TIN FROM THE KITCHEN

MITZ

DINGO X, 2 | **BARTON JONES WINES** DONNYBROOK, WA

KELLY
OWNERS: RICHARD AND SUE HATTERSLEY
PET HATE: LITTLE PUPPIES
FAVOURITE TOY: LEAVES WHICH SHE CARRIES IN HER MOUTH
OBSESSION: GETTING ATTENTION
FAVOURITE PASTIME: BEING PATTED
NAUGHTIEST DEED: STEALING THE SHOPPING OFF SOMEONE'S DOORSTEP

HUMPHREY
OWNERS: WILL AND REBECCA HATTERSLEY
PET HATE: VACUUM CLEANER
FAVOURITE TOY: WILL'S SOCKS
OBSESSION: CHASING KANGAROOS
NAUGHTIEST DEED: STEALING AND EATING 30 FROZEN SAUSAGES

WINSTON
OWNER: TOM HATTERSLEY
NAUGHTIEST DEED: NIBBLING PEOPLE'S FEET
OBSESSION: SORTING THROUGH THE RUBBISH BINS
PET HATE: VACUUM CLEANER
FAVOURITE FOOD: PIGS EARS
FAVOURITE PASTIME: CHEWING TOYS

BELGRAVIA WINES ORANGE, NSW | LABRADORS, 11, 5 & 4 MONTHS

OBSESSION: RUNNING
OWNER: JULIE HUTTON
PET HATE: HOT WEATHER
FAVOURITE TOY: HER OCTOPUS
FAVOURITE FOOD: BIG MEATY BONES
NAUGHTIEST DEED: CATCHING A SEAGULL SHE WAS CHASING
KNOWN ACCOMPLICES: CANDY AND HILARY, THE VINEYARD SHEEP

ZIPPY

GREYHOUND X, 3   BONKING FROG WINES NORTH BOYANUP, WA

MALLEE
FAVOURITE TOY: SOCKS
FAVOURITE PASTIME: ROAD TRIPS
OWNERS: MARTY AND JEN GRANSDEN
FAVOURITE FOOD: SPAGHETTI BOLOGNESE
PET HATE: BEING WOKEN UP BEFORE 10AM
OBSESSIONS: FOOD, ATTENTION, SOCKS AND SLEEP
NAUGHTIEST DEED: EATING AND DIGESTING A FIRE TRUCK

OTTO
OWNER: RUSS QUILTY
PET HATE: GETTING WASHED
NAUGHTIEST DEED: RAMMING PEOPLE IN THE CROTCH WITH HIS NOSE
FAVOURITE FOOD: LEFTOVERS FROM STAFF AT SMOKO
FAVOURITE TOY: BUZZ LIGHTYEAR THE MALTESE CROSS
OBSESSION: BARKING AT SIGNS FROM THE BACK OF THE UTE

CUMULUS ESTATE MOLONG, NSW | LABRADOR, 13 & BLUE HEELER X, 7

FAVOURITE FOOD: CHICKEN NECKS
OBSESSIONS: ICE CUBES AND WATER
NAUGHTIEST DEED: EATING HORSE POO
PET HATE: NOT BEING ALLOWED IN THE RESTAURANT
OWNERS: DUNCAN HEAD AND HONEY HIRANANDANI
FAVOURITE PASTIME: SWIMMING ANYWHERE HE CAN
FAVOURITE TOY: COLIN THE SOFT TOY RASTAFARIAN COW (DECEASED)

OLLIE

COCKER SPANIEL, 1 | **HEAFOD GLEN WINERY** HENLEY BROOK, WA

LUCKY

PET HATE: BATH TIME
OWNER: LORETTA BELL
KNOWN ACCOMPLICE: MAGGIE BELL
NAUGHTIEST DEEDS: KILLING A GUINEA PIG AND A COUPLE OF NORM'S CHOOKS
FAVOURITE PASTIME: RUNNING ON THE BEACH AT ROBE
OBSESSION: THE DARNED RABBITS UNDER THE SHED

BELLWETHER WINES COONAWARRA, SA   MALTESE X, 15

OWNER: MATT CARTER
OBSESSION: PLAYING FETCH
KNOWN ACCOMPLICES: JACINTA AND TESS
NAUGHTIEST DEED: MAKING A BED FROM A CASE OF TOILET PAPER IN THE STOREROOM
FAVOURITE PASTIME: SWIMMING IN THE DAM
FAVOURITE FOOD: ANYTHING FROM CHEF YOSHI
FAVOURITE TOY: ANY STICK – THE BIGGER THE BETTER
PET HATE: HAVING RIBBONS TIED TO HIM DURING DRESS-UP

WALDO

LABRADOR RETRIEVER, 8 | **BULONG ESTATE** YARRA JUNCTION, VIC

*"I like pigs. Dogs look up to us.
Cats look down on us.
Pigs treat us as equals."*

—— **WINSTON CHURCHILL**

THE TALE OF PINOT
AND THE GREAT PORK BARRELLING SCANDAL OF 2010

by Emma Moroney

Our story starts about four years ago when a couple of winsome winemakers at Holm Oak Winery, in Tassie's fertile Tamar Valley, decided it was time to add a furry friend to the fold. With only a touch of irony, they called him Pinot, for this was no light-bodied aroma of cherry-black fruit. No, 'man's best friend' was more of the full-flavoured variety. Farmyard overtones with bold tannic structure, Pinot was an animal not to be truffled with. Pinot is a pig.

Introduced to the Duffy family as a 'miniature pig' with only a short growing period, Pinot commenced winery life much the same as that most common of vineyard pets, the canine. With his pal Bella by his side, life on the vineyard was grand. The Cellar Door was his castle, the neighbours' vineyards his kingdom. Thanks to his penchant for party tricks (sitting on command, rolling over), a steady stream of loyal subjects kept him fed and entertained, and his sociable nature ensured his fame travelled far and wide.

Then came the White Sartorial Policy of 2010 and his reign as benevolent dictator came to an abrupt end. Forced into house arrest after a diplomatic disaster involving his muddy nose and a white cotton dress, Pinot d' Pig's dreams of inter-species cohabitation seemed lost. Never before had a pig had so much, to be reduced to so little.

But this was no ordinary pig. This was a pig with a platform. He'd go public!

In the winter of 2010 'Pinot d' Pig for PM' commenced with great enthusiasm (and a little too much alliteration) on Twitter (@PinotdPig). Thanks to the savvy skills of his campaign team and a talented ghostwriter, Pinot came out of the blocks trotters blazing. His first policy initiative? The Superfast Broadbean Proposal. Pow! Gaining momentum in the marginal seats of Bass and Braddon early, "Pinot d' Pig for PM" rolled out his next controversial policy initiative; 'Stop the Goats'. Pow pow!

This sent the Twitterverse into overdrive and really got him noticed. Riding high on a diet of fermented strawberries and apple cider, this not-so-little pig could smell victory.

And so could the faceless men. Pinot was a puppet in the making and it was time to pull some strings. Backroom meetings were held with key lobbyists. Forestry Tasmania got on board. Momentum was building. Pinot d' Pig could see the top job in his sights. Until disaster struck, in the form of a Sydney Morning Herald *exposé.*

The story of Pinot d' Pig's dirty pork barrelling scheme was picked up by every news outlet around the country. The faceless men had done it again. Pinot d' Pig's interparty politics had played him like a cheap Pianola and he was down for the count.

Not one for the backbench, Pinot immediately gave up politics and returned to Holm Oak where, inspired by the Indonesian wild cats that eat and excrete coffee beans before roasting them for human consumption, he is now happily cultivating his own line of bio-dynamic super-foods. A diffusion line of gourmet condiments is on the horizon if only he can stop Tim from eating his prized tomatoes.

You can follow Pinot d' Pig's regular musings on the state of Australian politics and more via Twitter @PinotdPig

EMMA MORONEY IS A TV PRODUCER (*CHANDON PICTURES*, *THE JESTERS*, *SMALL TIME GANGSTER*), FOOD BLOGGER (SURRYHILLS2010.WORDPRESS.COM) AND ALL-ROUND BOOZEHOUND. AN UNHEALTHY PENCHANT FOR GRAPE JUICE HAS SEEN HER TRAVEL FAR AND WIDE IN SEARCH OF THE PERFECT PINOT NOIR. HAVING OBSERVED THE DEBAUCHERY OF A TV CREW FILMING A WINE AND TRAVEL SHOW AS A CHILD IN THE 1980s, EMMA'S LIFELONG DREAM HAS BEEN TO COMBINE HER THREE GREAT LOVES AND PRODUCE HER OWN FOOD, WINE AND TRAVEL SHOW. COULD *WINE DOGS TV* FULFILL THIS DREAM? WATCH THIS SPACE…

KNOWN ACCOMPLICES:
BELLA, DARCY AND DEEVER
OBSESSION: BECOMING A CERTIFIED
ORGANIC VITICULTURAL WORKER
PET HATE: NOT GETTING ENOUGH FOOD
NAUGHTIEST DEED: ROLLING IN MUD THEN
GREETING CELLAR DOOR CUSTOMERS
OWNERS: TIM DUFFY AND REBECCA WILSON

PINOT

MINIATURE PIG, 4 | **HOLM OAK** ROWELLA, TAS

PEPPER

OWNER: CRAIG FENNELL
PET HATE: VACUUM CLEANER
KNOWN ACCOMPLICE: BAXTER
FAVOURITE FOOD: VEGEMITE TOAST CRUST FROM THE KIDS
FAVOURITE TOY: ENDLESS SUPPLY OF CHEAP TENNIS BALLS
NAUGHTIEST DEED: CHEWING UP CRAIG'S NEW WORK BOOTS
FAVOURITE PASTIME: FETCHING THE BALL NEAR CELLAR DOOR

BOAT O'CRAIGO HEALESVILLE, VIC | ROTTWEILER X, 2

OWNERS: TOM KEELAN AND REBECCA WILLSON
FAVOURITE TOY: OLD ADAM WINE BARREL BUNGS
PET HATE: HER ARCH NEMESIS – BREMERTON THE CAT
NAUGHTIEST DEED: SNEAKING INTO CELLAR DOOR FOR A PAT
FAVOURITE PASTIME: PLAYING CATCH WITH KIDS ON THE WINERY LAWN

CHARLIE

BORDER COLLIE, 10 | **BREMERTON WINES** LANGHORNE CREEK, SA

MANU

PET HATE: PINK COLLARS
OWNER: CHRISTINA PATTISON
FAVOURITE TOY: PUKU THE CAT
OBSESSIONS: SOCKS AND THE FEET INSIDE THEM
FAVOURITE PASTIMES: WRESTLING WITH RAFF AND LOOKING TOUGH
KNOWN ACCOMPLICES: BOOPH, PUKU, RAFF, BRUNO, JACK AND CHILLI
NAUGHTIEST DEED: EATING THE 2009 HUNTER VALLEY RISING STAR'S BEST SHOES

CHARTERIS WINE COMPANY CESSNOCK, NSW | ENGLISH STAFFORDSHIRE TERRIER, 2

OWNER: PJ CHARTERIS
FAVOURITE PASTIME: WATCHING ALL SUPER RUGBY GAMES EVERY WEEKEND
FAVOURITE FOODS: BISTECCA AND PINOT
KNOWN ACCOMPLICES: MANU, PUKU AND SIENNA
NAUGHTIEST DEED: DELETING MASTERCHEF FROM THE HARD DRIVE TO FIT MORE SUPER RUGBY ON IT
PET HATE: HAVING TO GET LIFTED INTO THE BACK OF THE UTE

BOOPH

RED CATTLE DOG, 12 | **CHARTERIS WINE COMPANY** CESSNOCK, NSW

BRUCE

OWNER: BRONNLEY CAHILL
PET HATE: HI-VIS CLOTHING
OBSESSION: BEING WITH OTHER PEOPLE AND DOGS
KNOWN ACCOMPLICE: HUBERT JACK JACK GREENSMITH III
FAVOURITE PASTIMES: RIDING IN THE TRACTOR AND CHEWING CANES
NAUGHTIEST DEED: STEALING BRONNLEY'S DINNER FROM THE KITCHEN

BROOKWOOD ESTATE COWARAMUP, WA | LABRADOR X, 2

TOWBY

OWNER: BRODIE HOWARD
OBSESSION: THE MOTORBIKE
PET HATE: BEING LEFT BEHIND
FAVOURITE PASTIME: ESCAPING THE WINERY TO BE A CATTLE DOG
FAVOURITE TOY: BARREL BUNGS
NAUGHTIEST DEED: LEADING MYLIE ASTRAY

MYLIE

OWNER: KATE HOWARD
FAVOURITE FOOD: CHEESE
FAVOURITE PASTIME: SWIMMING
PET HATE: HAVING HER EARS PLAYED WITH
OBSESSION: RETRIEVING AND BURYING EVERYTHING
NAUGHTIEST DEED: RETRIEVING THINGS THAT AREN'T HERS

KELPIE, 5 & CURLY-COATED RETRIEVER, 1 | **DUDLEY WINES** PENNESHAW, SA

LEXI

PET HATE: BATHS
OBSESSIONS: RATS AND MICE
FAVOURITE TOY: HUMPHREY B. BEAR
KNOWN ACCOMPLICES: JORDIE AND BANJO
OWNERS: PHILIP AND SANDRA GOLDRING
NAUGHTIEST DEED: ROLLING IN THE SMELLIEST COW PAT IN THE PADDOCK

HIDDEN RIVER ESTATE PEMBERTON, WA | JACK RUSSELL TERRIER, 7

OBSESSION: PAM
FAVOURITE FOOD: EGG FLIP
PET HATE: PAM GOING AWAY
FAVOURITE PASTIMES: FISHING AND BEING A FAFAFINI (LADY BOY)
NAUGHTIEST DEED: STEALING THE MAIN COURSE AT A WINERY FUNCTION
OWNERS: PAM AND HUGH HAMILTON

RODNEY

CURLY-COATED RETRIEVER, 9 | *HUGH HAMILTON WINES* McLAREN VALE, SA

SAM

FAVOURITE PASTIME: RUNNING THROUGH THE VINEYARD BESIDE THE CAR
OWNERS: HELEN AND STEVE MYLES
OBSESSION: TEDDY, THE STUFFED TOY
NAUGHTIEST DEED: STEALING DIRTY SOCKS
PET HATES: THE LAWN MOWER AND VACUUM CLEANER
KNOWN ACCOMPLICES: MISCHA, THE CATS, RASCAL AND CHARLIE

SUMBA

FAVOURITE TOY: OLD BONES
NAUGHTIEST DEED: DIGGING TO GET ATTENTION
FAVOURITE PASTIME: PLAYING WITH SCARLETT BURTON
FAVOURITE FOOD: LAMB SHANK
OBSESSION: BARKING AT SCHOOL KIDS WALKING PAST THE HOUSE
OWNERS: MATT AND RENEE BURTON

ELLIOTT

OBSESSION: TALKING
FAVOURITE TOY: SUMBA
FAVOURITE FOOD: SCARLETT'S LEFTOVER TOAST
NAUGHTIEST DEED: SNEAKING INTO THE HOUSE
PET HATE: THUNDERSTORMS
OWNERS: MATT AND RENEE BURTON
FAVOURITE PASTIME: HIS DAILY WALK

JACK

FAVOURITE FOOD: WHATEVER ELLIOTT'S EATING
OBSESSION: BEING OVER-AFFECTIONATE WITH PEOPLE
FAVOURITE PASTIME: EATING DINNER AS FAST AS POSSIBLE
PET HATE: GETTING INTO TROUBLE
NAUGHTIEST DEED: GETTING DIRTY
OWNERS: MATT AND RENEE BURTON

GOLDEN RETRIEVERS, 8, 10 & 6 | **GUNDOG ESTATE** POKOLBIN, NSW

WALLY

PET HATES: FLIES AND BATHS
OWNERS: THE HEYWOOD FAMILY
FAVOURITE TOY: THE NEIGHBOUR'S CAT
KNOWN ACCOMPLICES: JASMOND AND MINI
NAUGHTIEST DEED: SWIMMING IN THE EFFLUENT HOLDING POND THEN JUMPING INTO THE CAR
OBSESSION: FOLLOWING HIS OWNERS EVERYWHERE
FAVOURITE PASTIME: GETTING HIS OWNERS IN TROUBLE BY LEAVING 'PACKAGES' FOR THE GARDENER TO FIND

TALTARNI VINEYARDS MOONAMBEL, VIC | HEELER X, 6

OBSESSION: BIRDS IN THE NETS
NAUGHTIEST DEED: SNEAKY KISSES
OWNERS: TIM AND NARELLE CULLEN
FAVOURITE PASTIME: 'WORKING' IN THE VINES
PET HATES: BLOW FLIES AND BEING LEFT AT HOME
FAVOURITE TOY: ANYTHING THAT FLOATS OR SQUEAKS

DASH

KELPIE X, 10 | PAYNES RISE WINERY SEVILLE, VIC

MILLY

OWNER: KYM JENKE
OBSESSION: PLAYING WITH OTHER BOXERS
KNOWN ACCOMPLICES: CHAMPAGNE AND COOPER THE BOXERS
FAVOURITE PASTIME: GREETING VISITORS AT THE CELLAR DOOR
NAUGHTIEST DEED: CHASING KANGAROOS IN THE BACK VINEYARD
PET HATE: NOT BEING ABLE TO SLEEP IN FRONT OF THE CELLAR DOOR FIRE IN WINTER

JENKE VINEYARDS ROWLAND FLAT, SA | BOXER, 4

PUGSLEY

PET HATE: CABERNET THE WINE CAT
OWNERS: MICHAEL AND ANN BOURKE
FAVOURITE PASTIME: GETTING UNDERFOOT
FAVOURITE FOOD: ANYTHING HE CAN STEAL
NAUGHTIEST DEED: TRIPPING THE COOK OVER, LEADING TO AN AIRBORNE CHEESECAKE
OBSESSION: STANDING IN BETWEEN MICHAEL'S FEET

JESTER HILL WINES GLEN APLIN, QLD | TENTERFIELD TERRIER, 16

EADIE

OWNERS: THE SEXTON FAMILY
FAVOURITE FOOD: KANGAROO POO
FAVOURITE PASTIME: RUNNING WITH PHIL
NAUGHTIEST DEED: BAILING UP KANGAROOS
OBSESSION: KEEPING THE CHICKENS COMPANY
PET HATE: BEING TIED UP DURING A FULL MOON
KNOWN ACCOMPLICE: PIRATE, THE SHETLAND PONY

GIANT STEPS / INNOCENT BYSTANDER HEALESVILLE, VIC | LABRADOR, 4

OWNERS: SOUMAH
FAVOURITE FOOD: CRUNCHY CHIPS
OBSESSION: TRIPS IN ANY VEHICLE
PET HATES: BUNNIES AND MAGPIES
(MAGPIES SHOULD STAY IN TREES)
FAVOURITE TOY: SPIKY RUBBER BALL
NAUGHTIEST DEED: JUMPING IN DIRTY PUDDLES
FAVOURITE PASTIMES: BUNNY BITING AND BARKING AT WOMBATS

RUBY

CAIRN TERRIER, 3 | **SOUMAH OF YARRA VALLEY** GRUYERE, VIC

MOLLY

OWNER: MARSH ESTATE
FAVOURITE FOOD: EYE FILLET
PET HATE: CANNED DOG FOOD
KNOWN ACCOMPLICE: ENZO FROM TYRRELL'S
FAVOURITE TOY: SQUEAKY TOY (NOW SQUEAKLESS)
FAVOURITE PASTIME: CHASING TRACTORS, RABBITS AND FOXES
OBSESSION: ROLLING ON THE CARPET AFTER ROLLING IN COW DUNG
NAUGHTIEST DEED: BITING THROUGH A HOSE WHILE IT WAS PUMPING WINE

A TALKING DOG

by Andrew Marsh

"SO YOU'RE SAYING TO WAIT until tomorrow morning to adjust the nitrogen level?" I delicately ask, having already weighed out a small portion of diammonium phosphate to add to a red ferment.

"Of course, unless you wish to encourage an excess of acetate and ethyl fatty acid esters, impacting heavily on the aroma characteristics in such a new and progressive ferment. If you leave it for another 12 to 24 hours, you just may have a hope of a higher post-fermentation concentration of Malvidin-3-Glucoside," replies Molly.

"And what will that mean?" squinting my eyes and shaking my head in confusion.

"Well, obviously it will result in higher colour intensity and improved hue," states Molly.

"You amaze me yet again! How do you know so much about all this stuff?" I quiz.

"I read it all in your old university text books," she quips.

"I don't remember having text books at uni!" I reply.

"Yes, I had to take them out of their original plastic wrapping. By the way, what were you doing at university for all those years?"

"I was drinking ... and playing rugby ... and chasing girls ..."

"What about study?"

"What study?"

"Your winemaking!"

"What?"

"Nothing!"

I simply detest these conversations with Molly. I mean, I have a wife to keep me on the straight and narrow these days. The last thing I need is a talking bloody dog that never lets me out of her sight.

Oh, I almost forgot. My dog, Molly, can talk. No, really! She's a talking dog. She's like a female Mr Ed ... never shuts up. Highly intelligent, attractive, cool as a cucumber, insightful, courageous, reasonable, cautious ... pretty well all the traits I lack.

Molly just turned up one day, out of nowhere. She walked into the winery, sat at the door of the laboratory and stared at me. And stared. And stared.

"Good morning!" she finally blurted.

"S***!!" I yelled.

Molly simply kept her composure and in consequence to my off-colour expletive, threw me a withering look of contempt, as if to suggest that my lack of taste for a more appropriate adjective precluded further fraternisation.

"Don't panic. I'm a talking dog."

"No, I can see that. It's just that you said good morning. Every other talking dog I know lacks that quintessential sense of social grace."

"What?"

"Nothing."

So she's been with me ever since. She is named after Molly Deasy. The Deasy family owned all the land in my part of the Hunter Valley going back in time. Molly died at 105. She was a great old bird; I loved her.

Molly pretty well taught herself the winemaking game. Once I had taught her all I know ... over a cup of tea ... she took it upon herself to hone her skills in the magical world of wine. This has of course, led to a few sticky dilemmas.

Firstly, Molly is the only winemaking dog in Australia or New Zealand, making my job completely obsolete. Secondly, how do you market the fact that the lovable cellar door canine is the head of production for the entire company, and convince your loyal customers of its validity? Thirdly, I'd be stuffed without her! You see, she only talks to me. It's the typical movie scenario, where anyone who walks into the winery unannounced just happens to catch me mid-sentence talking to 'the dog'.

My friends are becoming increasingly concerned about my mental state. And that has nothing to do with this story. That simply stems from my involvement in the wine industry. No, they are concerned that I may be harbouring an invisible, make-believe friend, with whom I converse. Molly can hear and smell people coming a mile away, so she lays down as if she is asleep, leaving me with my back turned in conversation. So after too many years of this happening, I recently sat Molly down and told her that I'm going to blow the cover on the whole thing.

"How are you going to do that?" she demanded, "No-one will believe you."

"There's a new edition of Wine Dogs *coming out and I've been kindly asked to contribute a small story."*

"You wouldn't dare!" she stammered.

"Yes, I would."

"No, you wouldn't!"

"Yes, I would."

Molly sensed my overwhelming intent.

"Well, if you must" she insisted, "write that I'm really attractive and intelligent and cool as a cucumber and insightf..."

"What?"

"Nothing."

ANDREW MARSH IS THE WINEMAKER AT HUNTER VALLEY INSTITUTION MARSH ESTATE. A LOVABLE LARRIKIN KNOWN TO ALL WHO FREQUENT THE HUNTER SIMPLY AS 'MARSHY', HIS PASSION FOR WINE EXTENDS FAR AND WIDE. HE WRITES FOR SEVERAL PUBLICATIONS IN AUSTRALIA AND IS HIGHLY SOUGHT AFTER IN THE PUBLIC-SPEAKING ARENA. HIS ATTITUDE REFLECTS HIS NO-NONSENSE APPROACH TO WINEMAKING AND EDUCATING PEOPLE ON THE VIRTUES OF WINE. HIS CHEEKY GRIN AND BLACK SENSE OF HUMOUR MAKE FOR SOME INTERESTING TIMES AND HILARIOUS TALES.

MOCHA

OBSESSION: THE CAT NEXT DOOR
OWNERS: NIGEL AND KELLENE HARVEY
FAVOURITE FOOD: FREE-RANGE CHICKEN WINGS
FAVOURITE PASTIME: VISITING THE NEIGHBOURS AND WALKING THROUGH THEIR HOMES
NAUGHTIEST DEED: HELPING HERSELF TO SCRAPS
PET HATE: MORRIS THE CAT ENTERING HER YARD
KNOWN ACCOMPLICES: ETHAN, ART AND OSCAR HARVEY

VOYAGER ESTATE MARGARET RIVER, WA | MINIATURE GROODLE, 7

PET HATE: BEING WASHED
OWNER: ARNOLD VIERSMA
FAVOURITE FOOD: FRIED FISH
OBSESSION: RIDING IN THE CAR
NAUGHTIEST DEED: KILLING CHICKENS
KNOWN ACCOMPLICES: KASPA AND BOON
FAVOURITE PASTIME: HELPING WITH THE HANDPICKING

MAGGIE

BULL ARAB, 5 | **VOYAGER ESTATE** MARGARET RIVER, WA

FENG SHUI

PET HATE: BATHS
OWNER: SANDY THOMAS
FAVOURITE FOOD: CHEESE
OBSESSION: BARKING AT BIGGER DOGS FROM THE CAR
FAVOURITE TOY: BABE THE PIG
FAVOURITE PASTIME: CRABBING IN ROCK POOLS AT AUGUSTA BEACH
NAUGHTIEST DEED: EYEBALLING UNCLE COL'S GIANT KOI IN ITS POND

JACK

FAVOURITE PASTIME: BODYSURFING
OWNERS: HAYLEY AND DEON SANTICH
FAVOURITE TOY: SKIPPY THE KANGAROO
KNOWN ACCOMPLICE: UGLY THE CHICKEN
OBSESSION: FETCHING BALLS AND THONGS IN THE OCEAN
NAUGHTIEST DEED: SLEEPING ON THE BEDS AND LOUNGES
PET HATE: WHEN SOMEONE STANDS ON A CHAIR TO CHANGE A LIGHT BULB

VOYAGER ESTATE MARGARET RIVER, WA | RHODESIAN RIDGEBACK X, 3

OBSESSION: FOOD
NAUGHTIEST DEED: CHANGES DAILY
PET HATE: HAVING HIS PHOTO TAKEN
OWNERS: LYNDEN AND CHANTEL DAVIES
FAVOURITE TOY: WHATEVER EWAN IS PLAYING WITH
FAVOURITE PASTIME: STEALING FOOD AT ANY OPPORTUNITY
FAVOURITE FOODS: ANYTHING EDIBLE AND VARIOUS INEDIBLE THINGS

OSCAR

LABRADOR, 5 | *VOYAGER ESTATE* MARGARET RIVER, WA

HONEY
OWNERS: AMY TATE AND FAMILY
KNOWN ACCOMPLICES: ROCCO AND RUSTY
FAVOURITE PASTIME: SLEEPING ON THE BED
OBSESSION: PLASTIC LASER LIGHT MACHINE GUN
NAUGHTIEST DEED: EATING ELAINE'S CHOCOLATE STASH
PET HATE: KANGAROOS COMING TOO CLOSE TO THE HOUSE

ROCCO
OWNERS: AMY TATE AND FAMILY
OBSESSION: SUCKING CUDDLY TOYS
PET HATE: HAVING FLEA TREATMENT
FAVOURITE TOY: ICE-CREAM CONTAINERS
NAUGHTIEST DEED: WANDERING OFF TO SHOPPING CENTRES AND SCHOOLS TO FIND FOOD

VOYAGER ESTATE MARGARET RIVER, WA | SHIH TZU X, 4 & LABRADOR, 5

ROSY
OWNER: JUSTINE ALDRIDGE
PET HATE: OTHER DOGS, ESPECIALLY IF THEY ARE BIGGER THAN HER
FAVOURITE FOOD: ARROWROOT BISCUITS BROKEN INTO BITE-SIZED PIECES
OBSESSION: HAVING HER TUMMY TICKLED
NAUGHTIEST DEED: GIVING YOU A SWIPE WITH HER PAW IF YOU DON'T TICKLE HER TUMMY

TOM
OBSESSION: LICKING
OWNER: JUSTINE ALDRIDGE
PET HATE: THUNDERSTORMS
FAVOURITE PASTIME: EATING
NAUGHTIEST DEED: GETTING HIS HEAD STUCK THROUGH A FENCE, NEEDING TO BE SAWN OUT – TWICE
FAVOURITE FOOD: DECAYING BONES HE FINDS ON HIS WALKS

VOYAGER ESTATE MARGARET RIVER, WA | MALTESE X, 13

PET HATE: CATS
OWNER: CLAIRE TONON
OBSESSION: GIAC THE CAT
FAVOURITE PASTIME: CHASING CATS
NAUGHTIEST DEEDS: HIDING BONES IN
CLAIRE'S BED AND ESCAPING TO CHASE CATS
FAVOURITE FOOD: ANYTHING THE CAT IS EATING

RAFFI

MALTESE X, 10 | **VOYAGER ESTATE** MARGARET RIVER, WA

JEDDAH

PET HATE: THUNDER
OWNER: KATHRYN LOCKE
FAVOURITE TOY: MR PLATYPUS
NAUGHTIEST DEED: EATING 1080 POISON
OBSESSIONS: CHASING PARROTS AND FETCHING
FAVOURITE PASTIME: CHASING BALLS AND STICKS
KNOWN ACCOMPLICES: PONCHO AND THE CHOOKS

STELLA

OWNER: JAN STOCKER
FAVOURITE FOOD: CHICKEN NECKS
PET HATE: OTHER DOGS WALKING PAST
OBSESSION: BARKING AT PEOPLE IN HER STREET
NAUGHTIEST DEED: ESCAPING TO CHASE RABBITS
FAVOURITE PASTIME: WALKING AT THE BEACH WITH JAN

VOYAGER ESTATE MARGARET RIVER, WA | JACK RUSSELL TERRIER, 8

PET HATE: THUNDERSTORMS
OWNERS: STEVE AND MERRI JAMES
FAVOURITE PASTIMES: GOING TO THE BEACH AND SNOOZING ON THE DAY BED
NAUGHTIEST DEED: CATCHING A POSSUM
KNOWN ACCOMPLICES: STORMY AND WALTER
OBSESSION: CHASING POSSUMS ALONG THE FENCE

STELLA

RHODESIAN RIDGEBACK, 10 | **VOYAGER ESTATE** MARGARET RIVER, WA

KASPA

OWNER: DUTCHY
PET HATE: RUNNING
KNOWN ACCOMPLICES: ZEPHYR, GELERT, BOON AND MAGGIE
FAVOURITE PASTIME: CHECKING AROUND THE VINES FOR MICE
OBSESSION: BITING WATER FROM TAPS
NAUGHTIEST DEED: POOING ON THE LAWNS

VOYAGER ESTATE MARGARET RIVER, WA | BLUE HEELER X, 9

MAGGIE
PET HATE: THE CHOOKS
OWNER: LYNDEN GAMAGE
FAVOURITE FOOD: CHICKEN
NAUGHTIEST DEED: RUNNING AWAY
FAVOURITE PASTIME: CHASING HORSES
OBSESSION: HANGING OUT WITH BRUCE
KNOWN ACCOMPLICES: BRUCE, ROGER, LISSA AND PADDY

ROGER
FAVOURITE TOY: LISSA
OWNER: LYNDEN GAMAGE
OBSESSION: STALKING THE CATS
FAVOURITE PASTIME: GOING IN THE CAR
NAUGHTIEST DEED: CHASING KANGAROOS
KNOWN ACCOMPLICE: SANCHEZ THE DONKEY

WEST HIGHLAND TERRIERS, 3 & 4 | **VOYAGER ESTATE** MARGARET RIVER, WA

PEDRO
OBSESSION: FOOD
OWNER: GEOFF KNEEBONE
NAUGHTIEST DEED: BITING GEOFF'S DAUGHTER'S BOYFRIEND
PET HATE: GETTING HIS PAWS WET
FAVOURITE FOOD: ANY CRUMBS ON THE KITCHEN FLOOR
FAVOURITE PASTIME: SLEEPING IN HIS BASKET IN THE SUN

OLLIE
OBSESSION: SOCKS
OWNER: GEOFF KNEEBONE
FAVOURITE PASTIME: GOING TO THE VET
PET HATES: KITTENS AND VACUUM CLEANERS
FAVOURITE FOOD: DUCK EGGS FRESH FROM THE NEST
FAVOURITE TOYS: PEDRO AND ANYTHING ELSE THAT SQUEAKS

VOYAGER ESTATE MARGARET RIVER, WA | CHIHUAHUA, 9 & MALTELIER, 5

PET HATE: PARTIES
FAVOURITE TOY: JIMMY THE CAT
FAVOURITE FOOD: LAMB SHANKS
OWNERS: MARNIE AND MARK KELLY
OBSESSION: CHEWING, CHEWING AND CHEWING
FAVOURITE PASTIMES: WALKING AND SWIMMING
NAUGHTIEST DEED: CHEWING THROUGH THE FOXTEL CABLE

COCO

LABRADOR, 6 | **VOYAGER ESTATE** MARGARET RIVER, WA

RAHNI
OBSESSION: THE TRACTOR
OWNER: FRANCINE DAVIES
PET HATE: BEING LEFT AT HOME
FAVOURITE TOYS: ROPE AND BALL
FAVOURITE PASTIME: HANGING OUT WITH BONO ON THE FRONT PORCH

BONO
OWNER: FRANCINE DAVIES
FAVOURITE FOOD: MEATY BONES
FAVOURITE PASTIME: CHASING BIRDS
NAUGHTIEST DEED: VISITING TABLE 12
PET HATES: GETTING WET AND BEING LEFT AT HOME
OBSESSIONS: BIRDS, SQUEAKY TOYS AND SHADOWS

VOYAGER ESTATE MARGARET RIVER, WA | BORDER COLLIE, 4 & KELPIE X, 13

OWNER: DAVID SHERIDAN
FAVOURITE FOOD: KANGAROO
FAVOURITE TOY: SOCCER BALL
FAVOURITE PASTIME: PLAYING
WITH HER TAIL AT THE BEACH
OBSESSION: CHASING HER TAIL
NAUGHTIEST DEED: STANDING
ON ALL THE FLOWERS AT VOYAGER

BONNIE

PEMBROKE CORGI, 8 | *VOYAGER ESTATE* MARGARET RIVER, WA

EILEEN
THE WIREHAIRED FOX TERRIER

by Greg Duncan Powell

THERE ARE SOME DOG BREEDS that you are destined to have. They stick in your head and haunt your dreams until one day they enter your life and then it is as if they were always meant to be there. On school days in the early 1970s I used to come home and watch a show on TV called The Ghost and Mrs Muir. *It was about a widow, Mrs Muir, and her strange unrequited relationship with Captain Daniel Gregg, a ghost. But the star of the show was neither, it was a terrier named Scruffy. I was unacquainted with Scruffy's breeding or pedigree but was very much taken with his manner, his energy, his intelligence and his tremendous acting ability. Episodes of the show where Scruffy didn't play a role just had no appeal and he became my ideal of canine-inity.*

Wind time forward 40 odd years and I find myself in the market for a dog of the small terrier type and discover that the dog that I had in my head all those years was a wirehaired fox terrier.

'Wires' – as they're known by aficionados – are no longer a popular breed, as I soon discovered. I embarked on an Australia-wide wire search which eventually led me to the train station carpark in the pretty Murray River town of Cobram on a Thursday afternoon in September. That was the half-way point between me and the breeder and that was where I first laid eyes on Eileen. The dog I'd had in my head all those years was the one I was looking at. Spooky. We spent that evening and night in a caravan park in Rutherglen while they were judging the Rutherglen Wine Show across the way – a fortuitous start for a wine dog.

Meanwhile at home, as the yet unnamed Eileen and I drove back up the Hume Highway, the family were throwing around names. Our four-year-old was going for Princess or Liana or Elexa or all three together, but the rest of us were thinking outside the confines of Barbie DVDs and one name stuck – a name that was popular back in the days when wires were as popular as schnauzers – Eileen.

A dog's personality is a blend. There are the inherited things – the characteristics of the breed – and the personality traits and quirks unique to the dog. With new dogs of unfamiliar breeds differentiating the two can be tricky. Eileen was three months old then and already appeared mature – a blend of brave terrier and sooky lap dog. She took to our house as if she were paying the mortgage and determined to use any bed for her own purposes. She made it very clear she would be an inside and an outside dog as she pleased. As far as toilet training goes she seemed to get the hang of all that very quickly and appeared to be intelligent, gentle with the kids but also an excellent hunter – all apparently true to form for a wirehaired fox terrier.

"Once you've had a wire you can never have another breed" was what Eileen's breeder assured me and it rang in my ears as I proudly watched her become fluent in the nuances of the English language. But there was a flipside. She could be the most wilful, naughtiest, terrible terrier imaginable. A bit of research excused her. It wasn't her personality at work; it was her breeding, which had a tendency to exert its individuality at inopportune moments. This was a comfort as she applied her inherited genes to socks, shoes, smelly chewables and various dead and decaying things.

But there was one character trait of which the dog breed books said nothing – she seemed to like music. She would drape herself over my shoulder as I noodled with the guitar on the couch. She would attempt to share my lap with my Stratocaster, her head bumping against the whammy bar and her hair muffling the strings. Obviously, even my music was soothing to a young pup ripped off the farm and placed in a family of wild young children.

But there was more to it than that. She loved dancing in the kitchen with the kids, going to sleep in the car with the CD player turned up to ten and showed more respect for musical gear than other bits of our property. But the real proof that Eileen was a bit special came the day that my band, "The Swinging Gonads", was rehearsing in the garage. "The Gonads" are not death metal by any stretch but a band with a drummer in a tin shed is loud for a human and especially loud for a dog, But not this dog. As we launched into the first number she didn't head for the doors as every other pooch I had known had done, but moved closer to the guitar amp and sat in front absorbing the wattage in her small canine frame.

Next song she walked over to the bass player's amp and tried to climb inside. I'd seen something similar in a previous band but not with a dog. That band had a particularly vigorous drummer whose bass drum had a tendency to march across the room into the (usually) small audience. The solution to this problem came from a 'fan' who would lie with his head inside the bass drum thus negating the need for sandbags to hold the drum in place. We thought he was crazy (and he clearly was) and while Eileen didn't do anything nearly as silly as that, she did seem to prefer music to her hearing. When we practised our version of Cream's 'Sunshine of Your Love' (as every band must do) it was as if – like most humans – she already had it in her DNA. I don't know if a feisty terrier can groove but she was doing a pretty good impression.

And so she has become a regular at the Gonads band rehearsals. There are certain songs, and sounds she likes more than others, and her taste is pretty good: she prefers my Gretsch over the Telecaster, loves a wah wah solo, enjoys the smell of hot valve amps and gets excited when guitars are removed from their cases. Eileen is obviously too intelligent and too small to be a roadie but apparently wirehaired fox terriers can be trained to do anything, and The Swinging Gonads are currently in need of a good sound engineer...

GREG DUNCAN POWELL HAS BEEN WRITING ABOUT WINE AND OTHER DRINKS FOR MOST OF HIS ADULT LIFE. CURRENTLY HE IS DRINKS EDITOR FOR *MASTERCHEF*, PLAYING GUITAR WITH 'THE SWINGING GONADS' AND WRITING LOADS OF BOOKS. HIS MOST RECENT WORKS ARE *BEER – A GAUGE FOR ENTHUSIASTS* (MURDOCH BOOKS) AND *GLOVEBOX GUIDE TO WINE TOURING*. WWW.GREGDUNCANPOWELL.COM.AU

PRINCE WILLIAM AKA BILLY

FAVOURITE FOOD: CHICKEN
OWNERS: RALPH AND VAL JONES
PET HATE: HAVING HIS NAILS CLIPPED
FAVOURITE PASTIME: GETTING UP TO MISCHIEF
FAVOURITE TOY: STUFFED CHICKEN WITH BELL
NAUGHTIEST DEED: RUINING A LEATHER SLIPPER
KNOWN ACCOMPLICES: HIS HALF-BROTHER AND HALF-SISTER

KELLERMEISTER LYNDOCH, SA | CHIHUAHUA, 8 MONTHS

DODGER

FAVOURITE TOY: UGG BOOTS
FAVOURITE PASTIME: CHASING THINGS, EVEN IF THEY'RE NOT REALLY THERE
OBSESSIONS: DUCKS, HIS OWN NETHER REGIONS AND KIDS ON SKATEBOARDS
NAUGHTIEST DEED: EATING RAY-BANS, A RUG AND CHRISTMAS DECORATIONS
KNOWN ACCOMPLICES: MONTY THE AIREDALE TERRIER AND COOPER THE KELPIE
OWNERS: TOBY YAP AND PENNY BOOTHMAN

LANGMEIL WINERY TANUNDA, SA | HUNGARIAN VIZSLA, 8 MONTHS

OWNER: TIM FOLLETT
FAVOURITE FOOD: METWURST
FAVOURITE TOY: SQUEAKY PIG
OBSESSION: TUMMY SCRATCHES
NAUGHTIEST DEED: DIGGING HOLES
KNOWN ACCOMPLICE: SISTER CHARLIE
FAVOURITE PASTIMES: EATING AND CHEWING SHOES

JESS

BORDER COLLIE, 4 MONTHS | **LAKE BREEZE** LANGHORNE CREEK, SA

FLYNN

FAVOURITE TOY: STRIPEY CUSHION
PET HATES: MAGPIES, HARES AND FOXES
FAVOURITE FOODS: CAT FOOD AND CHICKEN
OWNERS: INGA LIDUMS AND DAVE NEYLE
FAVOURITE PASTIMES: PADDLING IN THE DAM AND RIDING IN THE UTE WITH DAVE
OBSESSIONS: BARKING AT THE MOON ON QUIET NIGHTS AND CHASING HARES
NAUGHTIEST DEED: CHEWING DAVE'S SUNGLASSES, WALLET AND MOBILE PHONE

LOBETHAL ROAD WINES MOUNT TORRENS, SA | FOX TERRIER X, 7

OWNER: WAYNE HARDING
FAVOURITE FOOD: CHICKEN
FAVOURITE PASTIME: SLEEPING
NAUGHTIEST DEED: DIGGING HOLES
OBSESSION: WAITING FOR WAYNE TO GET HOME
KNOWN ACCOMPLICES: MURRAY'S BEER DRINKERS

LOU LOU

BULL ARAB X, 3 | **PORT STEPHENS WINERY** BOBS FARM, NSW

BUSTER

OWNER: DRU RESCHKE
PET HATE: THE WORD "BATH"
FAVOURITE TOY: DRU'S SOCKS
OBSESSION: TRICKS FOR TREATS
NAUGHTIEST DEED: WEEING ON A CUSTOMER'S FOOT WHEN HE WAS A PUPPY
FAVOURITE PASTIME: DOING HIS RANGE OF TRICKS FOR VISITORS

KOONARA WINES PENOLA, SA | JACK RUSSELL TERRIER X, 6

LARRY AKA 'FAT-LAZ'

OWNER: DAVID BICKNELL
FAVOURITE FOOD: BABY RABBIT
PET HATES: THUNDER AND FIREWORKS
FAVOURITE PASTIMES: GOING TO WORK AND LETTING OFF UNDER DAVID'S DESK
OBSESSION: BEGGING FOR FOOD IN THE RESTAURANT
NAUGHTIEST DEEDS: EATING ALL OF ANGUS' SIX CHICKENS AND LEAVING DEPOSITS IN THE MIDDLE OF THE WINERY

STAFFORDSHIRE TERRIER, 12 | **OAKRIDGE WINES** COLDSTREAM, VIC

LARA

OBSESSION: PLAYING STICK
KNOWN ACCOMPLICE: PUSS
OWNERS: GREG AND NATALA FLYNN
PET HATE: BEING SPOKEN TO GRUFFLY
NAUGHTIEST DEED: LEAPING ONTO CAR BONNETS
FAVOURITE FOOD: THE STINKIEST CARCASS SHE CAN FIND
FAVOURITE PASTIME: PLAYING WITH STICKS WITH CUSTOMERS

FLYNNS WINES HEATHCOTE, VIC | KELPIE, 9

BRUTUS AKA CHALK

OWNER: ALLAN NALDER
OBSESSION: TENNIS BALLS
FAVOURITE TOY: TENNIS BALLS
NAUGHTIEST DEEDS: DESTROYING TENNIS BALLS AND ALLAN'S GUCCI LOAFERS
FAVOURITE PASTIME: CHEWING TENNIS BALLS
KNOWN ACCOMPLICES: CAESAR AND THE GOATS

CAESAR AKA CHEESE

OWNER: ALLAN NALDER
NAUGHTIEST DEED: PLAYING ROUGH WITH ALLAN'S MUM'S CHOOKS
KNOWN ACCOMPLICES: BRUTUS AND ALLAN
FAVOURITE FOOD: COOKED LOCAL SAUSAGES
OBSESSION: CHASING ANYTHING WITH FEATHERS
PET HATES: CHAINSAWS AND OTHER LOUD NOISES

LABRADORS, 9 | **HELEN'S HILL ESTATE** COLDSTREAM, VIC

DASHA

OWNER: RON BROWN
PET HATE: SEA WATER
FAVOURITE FOOD: CHOCOLATE
FAVOURITE TOYS: SOFA CUSHIONS
NAUGHTIEST DEED: DEPOSITING
RABBITS ON THE LIVING ROOM FLOOR
OBSESSIONS: RABBITS OR ANYTHING THAT MOVES
FAVOURITE PASTIME: SNIFFING AROUND THE VINEYARDS

MAVERICK WINES BAROSSA VALLEY, SA | JACK RUSSELL TERRIER, 3

EDELWEISS ERNIE

by Ben Canaider

MY MOTHER HAS ALWAYS BEEN a great exponent of the pathetic fallacy. That's the notion of ascribing human emotions to things which aren't human, like rocks or clouds or animals. She is brilliant at it, and believes that if animals can have human feelings they should be treated like humans. Hard hearts, cruel hearts, don't believe in this emotional nonsense. Of course not. Everyone reading this book, however, would be a dead-set believer in the pathetic fallacy idea.

It can be taken to extremes, though, as I discovered when I turned 12, and when Mum brought home a posh, pedigreed German Shepherd. Ernie. Edelweiss Ernie, as his kennel warranty put it.

He was a fabulously handsome if somewhat shaky puppy. Not uncoordinated like big dogs in their puppy form can be; but shaky as in traumatised. He'd been recently shot at. The shot missed, but Ernie was left unhinged. His kennel owner had sold Ernie but the cheque had bounced. The kennel owner went around to the bouncee's farm to shoot the dog. BANG. A fight followed, the police came, and so on and so forth.

My mother did goody-goody pro bono *work for a dog charity. She was invariably the person they called when they had an unhinged dog. We'd had plenty of such dogs during my childhood. There was an Afghan Hound (Demis – named after Demis Roussos... don't ask me why...) who only wanted to run in a straight line.*

There was Lurch the Weimaraner who had to howl (or sing, as mum put it). And there was also a black Labrador who thought she was one of the Bronte sisters reincarnated – Emily. Golly, she was a tragic. Kept trying to drown herself. But Ernie was the pick of them, and had the greatest effect on my young life.

Because Ernie now became my equal. Or, perhaps, I became his *equal. My mother's reckless indulgence for me was now split in two. Half for me, and half for Ernie. Sometimes though, it felt more like 40/60 – and definitely in the dog's favour.*

Our – the family's – diet changed. Car travel changed. Everything changed. All thanks to Ernie.

My mother started to cook again. But for Ernie. She made him wonderful beef stews, and chicken dishes. Lots of couscous and sausage. Rice dishes. Dad and I ate like horses, living on alfalfa sprouts.

The front passenger seat was taken out of the Volkswagen so that Ernie could sit more easily – riding up the front with his mother. I sat on the back seat, without a window to wind down...

Weekends centred around Ernie's exercise and leisure regime. Mum and Dad would drive him off to staggeringly impressive bits of our mountain-top geography so he could prance about like a prince of a German duchy. This meant I had to walk to everything. Football. Friends. Fun. All on foot. Oh, did I mention we lived in the mountains?

If I had a sore tooth I was told it was a growing pain. If Ernie looked in anything less than picture postcard condition, then he'd be rushed to the vet by medi-vac air-ambulance. Being my mother's son, though, I couldn't defeat the gene. There was something about Ernie. And I came to love him. I tried to not let it show.

And this is how my adolescence went. Hours became days and days turned into weeks and in and out of years until I got home from university one day and saw a sign posted on the laundry door – or Ernie's room.

"Do not disturb. Ernie is depressed."

I opened the door. He was on his day bed, with his jaw resting on his crossed-over front paws. His eyes were sort of milky, and he didn't even look up at me – not a glance. Not a jot of the sort of brotherly look he'd been giving me for eight years. "Hi Ben, you're home, do you want to run around out the back for a bit?"

Ernie was depressed. He was 8. His back legs had recently been a bit wobbly. Early stages of dog arthritis, his medical team had diagnosed. Had he seen the writing on the wall? If you can't be 100% German Shepherd why bother being a German Shepherd at all? Why bother living?

If you can't climb into your customised German car and be chauffeured around to impressive bits of mountain top where on you can do canine impersonations of Ludwig II at exercise, why go on?

Ernie died a few weeks later. There were some other health issues, it proved. He died, I moved out of home, my mother seem to strangely age. My father kept putting acres of alfalfa shoots into his cheese sandwiches. He'd come to quite like the stuff. Or maybe he was remembering Ernie.

They got another dog about a year later, but it only ever barked at me, as if I were a complete stranger. It was just a dog. But my brother had been a German Shepherd.

BEN CANAIDER IS A WINE AND DRINKS WRITER. HE IS THE AUTHOR OF NINE BOOKS, INCLUDING *THE PERFECT GLASS OF WINE* AND *CUISINE DU MOI* — THE LATTER A CELEBRITY CHEF SPOOF.

PET HATE: THE VET
OWNER: LISA THOMSON
FAVOURITE FOOD: LAMB SHANK
FAVOURITE TOY: MOUSE SOFT TOY
OBSESSION: FINDING LOST THINGS
FAVOURITE PASTIME: BEING WITH LISA
NAUGHTIEST DEED: ROUNDING UP THE NEIGHBOUR'S SHEEP

VINNIE

KELPIE, 5 | **STONE BRIDGE WINES** CLARE, SA

BUZZ

OBSESSION: BIRDS
FAVOURITE PASTIME: BEING A WORRY WART
NAUGHTIEST DEED: SORTING OUT THE RUBBISH
OWNER: ROB QUENBY
FAVOURITE TOY: ROB'S UTE
FAVOURITE FOOD: KEV'S LUNCH BOX

WEST CAPE HOWE WINES MOUNT BARKER, WA | BORDER COLLIE X, 8

IAIN

OWNER: VIRGINIA WILLCOCK
PET HATES: BANGS, CRASHES AND MOTORS
FAVOURITE PASTIME: HANGING WITH VIRGINIA
NAUGHTIEST DEED: RIPPING APART CUSHIONS WITH AUSTIN AND SLEEPING IN A PILE OF FLUFF
OBSESSION: HIS FLUFFY BIG COUSIN AUSTIN THE LABRADOR

VASSE FELIX COWARAMUP, WA | STAFFORDSHIRE BULL TERRIER, 10

MISSISSIPPI

PET HATE: THUNDER
NAUGHTIEST DEED: RAIDING GRANDMA'S PANTRY
OBSESSIONS: FOOD AND ROLLING IN UNMENTIONABLE THINGS
OWNERS: NATHAN AND SARAH BERESFORD
FAVOURITE PASTIMES: ROLLING IN UNMENTIONABLE THINGS AND (FORTUNATELY) SWIMMING IN THE DAM
FAVOURITE FOOD: ANYTHING IN LARGE QUANTITIES

MINNESOTA

PET HATE: GETTING CARSICK
FAVOURITE TOY: BIG DOG'S TAIL
OWNERS: JOHN AND JENNY HORGAN
FAVOURITE FOOD: SOMETHING DISGUSTING THAT HAS BEEN LONG DEAD AND BURIED
OBSESSION: SWINGING ON BIG DOGS' TAILS
FAVOURITE PASTIME: CHASING RABBITS AND GUINEA FOWL
NAUGHTIEST DEED: SNEAKING INTO THE GRANDCHILDREN'S BEDS

LABRADOR, 14 & JACK RUSSELL TERRIER, 7 | **SALITAGE WINERY** PEMBERTON, WA

FLUFFY

PET HATE: MAGPIES
OWNER: MILLICENT GIBSON
FAVOURITE PASTIME: WIND SURFING
FAVOURITE TOY: BLUE HIPPOPOTAMUS
KNOWN ACCOMPLICES: ROSIE AND ZENA
OBSESSION: GETTING A THOUSAND PATS A DAY
FAVOURITE FOOD: DOG BISCUITS HOME-MADE BY MILLICENT

WORD OF MOUTH WINES ORANGE, NSW   MOODLE, 4

INDI
FAVOURITE FOOD: PIGS EARS
OWNERS: TANYA AND MICHAEL OLINDER
PET HATES: CORKS POPPING AND MICROWAVES
FAVOURITE TOY: GRANDMA'S GARDENING SHOES
NAUGHTIEST DEED: RUNNING INTO A FAMOUS CHEESE SHOP IN TASSIE AND PEEING ON THE FLOOR
FAVOURITE PASTIME: GOING DOWN SLIPPERY SLIDES

LILA
PET HATE: COMING BACK WHEN CALLED
OWNERS: TANYA AND MICHAEL OLINDER
OBSESSION: GREETING EVERYONE SHE SEES
FAVOURITE TOY: GRANDMA'S HOSE FITTINGS
FAVOURITE FOOD: TIGGER THE CAT'S DINNER
FAVOURITE PASTIME: ROLLING IN SMELLY THINGS
NAUGHTIEST DEED: CHEWING A LEXUS' LEATHER DOOR TRIM

ENGLISH STAFFORDSHIRE BULL TERRIERS, 2 | SHAW VINEYARD ESTATE MURRUMBATEMAN, NSW

BIDDI

OWNERS: THE CHAMBERS FAMILY
FAVOURITE FOODS: BACON AND CAT FOOD
KNOWN ACCOMPLICES: MAX, JOEL AND WHISPER THE CAT
FAVOURITE PASTIMES: CHASING RABBITS AND GOING FOR A JOG
OBSESSIONS: FLIES, MICE AND CHASING THE SHEEP DOGS OFF THE VERANDAH
NAUGHTIEST DEED: ROLLING IN SOMETHING DEAD THEN SLEEPING ON THE COUCH
PET HATES: SMALL WHITE DOGS AND THE SHEEP DOGS COMING ONTO THE VERANDAH

LAKE MOODEMERE VINEYARDS RUTHERGLEN, VIC | JACK RUSSELL TERRIER, 12

MAXIMUS

OBSESSION: FOOD
PET HATE: MARCH FLIES
FAVOURITE TOYS: BIG AND LITTLE TED
OWNERS: STEVE AND KAREN MASTERS
KNOWN ACCOMPLICES: CHUCKIE AND BRUNO
FAVOURITE PASTIME: SLEEPING ON THE LEATHER LOUNGE FOLLOWED BY A REFRESHING DIP IN THE DAM
NAUGHTIEST DEED: PLAYING TOO ROUGH WITH GUINEA FOWL

LOST LAKE WINES PEMBERTON, WA | LABRADOR, 4

OWNER: JIM SWIFT
OBSESSION: WHEELS
FAVOURITE TOY: SQUEAKY TOYS
PET HATES: SUMMER AND OTHER DOGS
FAVOURITE PASTIME: LOOKING FOR BUNNIES
FAVOURITE FOOD: BONES – THE BIGGER, THE BETTER
NAUGHTIEST DEED: STEALING A PACKET OF SCHMACKOS
FROM THE NEIGHBOURS' PANTRY AND BRINGING IT HOME

LACHLAN

BLUE HEELER, 11 | **PRINTHIE WINES** MOLONG, NSW

SOPHIE
OBSESSION: BUNG CRICKET
OWNER: JEREMY MAXWELL
PET HATE: BAROSSA SHIRAZ
FAVOURITE PASTIME: TENNIS
FAVOURITE FOODS: RABBIT AND PAL
FAVOURITE TOYS: ROCKS AND TENNIS BALLS

OLIVE
OWNER: LEWIS MAXWELL
FAVOURITE FOOD: RABBITS
PET HATE: RABBITS ON THE WRONG SIDE OF THE FENCE
FAVOURITE PASTIME: HUNTING
OBSESSION: CHASING RABBITS

PET HATE: THUNDER
FAVOURITE TOY: SPRINKLERS
KNOWN ACCOMPLICE: OSCAR THE CAT
OWNERS: BITTEN AND KARSTEN PEDERSEN
FAVOURITE PASTIME: SUNDAY DRIVES WITH KARSTEN IN THE 1970'S ROLLS ROYCE
FAVOURITE FOODS: RAW MEAT AND BISCUITS
OBSESSIONS: WATER HOSES AND SPRINKLERS
NAUGHTIEST DEED: WETTING VISITORS' CAR TYRES

LEVI

KELPIE, 5 | **MALCOLM CREEK WINERY** KERSBROOK, SA

NILLO

OWNER: CAMERON LEITH
KNOWN ACCOMPLICE: JINSKY THE CAT
FAVOURITE TOYS: BALLS, CORKS AND FOOTBALLS
OBSESSION: FETCHING BALLS, CORKS, FOOTBALLS, ANYTHING...
FAVOURITE PASTIME: CHASING BIRDS AWAY FROM THE VINEYARD
PET HATES: VISITORS NOT THROWING THE BALL AND PESKY BIRDS
NAUGHTIEST DEED: SUFFERING KIDNEY FAILURE AFTER EATING A BUCKET OF FERMENTED GRAPES

PASSING CLOUDS MUSK, VIC | KELPIE, 2

FAVOURITE FOOD: TINNED SARDINES
NAUGHTIEST DEED: CHASING CHOOKS
OWNERS: FIONA WELLER AND JULIAN ALLPORT
OBSESSIONS: HUMAN CONTACT AND SUNSHINE
KNOWN ACCOMPLICES: CHILLI FROM DELAMERE VINEYARD AND JACK FROM DICKENS CIDER
FAVOURITE TOYS: VINE CROWNS AND BLOW FLIES
FAVOURITE PASTIME: AGITATING NEIGHBOURING COWS

OTTO

WEIMARANER, 2 | **MOORES HILL ESTATE** SIDMOUTH, TAS

SPUDD
PET HATE: HAVING A BATH
FAVOURITE FOOD: SCHMACKOS
OBSESSION: HUNTING RABBITS
OWNERS: JOEL AND SARAH ALLAN
KNOWN ACCOMPLICE: RUBY HARPER
FAVOURITE PASTIME: SLEEPING ON THE BEAN BAG
NAUGHTIEST DEED: EATING JOEL'S DAD'S CAMPER SHOES

CLEO
PET HATE: LIZARDS
FAVOURITE TOY: TENNIS BALL
OBSESSION: STEALING OTHER DOGS' TOYS
KNOWN ACCOMPLICES: MATILDA AND YOGI
OWNERS: CORALIE GARNIER AND MAT LEWIS
FAVOURITE PASTIME: CHASING DUCKS AND GOATS
NAUGHTIEST DEED: EATING AN ENTIRE BAG OF DOG BISCUITS

PET HATE: CATS
FAVOURITE TOY: BALLS
FAVOURITE FOOD: GOOD-OS
NAUGHTIEST DEED: CHASING COWS
KNOWN ACCOMPLICES: YOGI AND CLEO
OWNERS: LIZ DAWSON AND SHANE WEBB
FAVOURITE PASTIME: SLEEPING ON THE COUCH

MATILDA

STAFFORDSHIRE BULL TERRIER, 5 | **FERMOY ESTATE** WILYABRUP, WA

ARCHIMEDES
FAVOURITE FOOD: CHEESE
FAVOURITE TOY: BLUE SPIKY BALL
OWNERS: CONOR AND HEIDI VAN DER REEST
NAUGHTIEST DEED: KILLING TWELVE CHICKENS
OBSESSION: BEING CLOSE TO CONOR AND HEIDI
FAVOURITE PASTIMES: PLAYING CHASE AND GETTING PATS

PHOEBE
OBSESSION: PLAYING BALL
FAVOURITE PASTIME: PLAYING FETCH
PET HATE: BEING COVERED WITH A BLANKET
OWNERS: CONOR AND HEIDI VAN DER REEST
FAVOURITE FOOD: ANYTHING THAT ARKIE HAS
NAUGHTIEST DEED: HELPING ARKIE EAT THOSE CHICKENS

JOKER

by Matthew Jukes

A LITTLE TERRIER WAS BROUGHT TO THE OLD RECTORY aged two months old as a gift to Antony after he had undergone some very serious heart surgery. This little chap, son of Moley, a Sealyham/Jack Russell cross and a father of no name who was a pure Sealyham, was the result of a union match-made by the venerable John Brake, who breeds so many characterful terriers that he couldn't remember who in fact the father was who did the glorious deed.

Anyway, this odd-looking black-and-white puppy's job was to encourage Antony to get out and about walking around the glorious surroundings of the Wylye Valley, in Wiltshire, in order to build up his strength again after he had spent so much time in hospital. This puppy didn't seem that interested in helping Antony's recovery, preferring to tear around, ignoring his owner and reducing Antony to the most exasperated (and accurate) impressions of Basil Fawlty that I have ever seen – not good for the heart, we all whispered, sniggering.

He was named Joker after a lot of deliberation, because all of the family's terriers had names with gaming connections – Scrabble's ghost (possibly the naughtiest and most fearless of Joker's ancestors) was certainly looking down from on high, applauding every one of Joker's impossibly frustrating deeds. You could guarantee that Antony would shout 'Joker' at the top of his voice several times an hour and almost incessantly on our various walks around the Iron Age hill forts of Battlesbury and Scratchbury Camps.

The joke was on us though because Joker has confounded us all with his peculiar, hilarious, Antony-combusting exploits. He had a mind of his own, preferring to sit on the front doorstep or trot around outside rather than lounge near the fire and he often disappeared for hours on end and we were none the wiser about where he'd been.

Strolling through the village one day, a man with a dog informed Antony that Joker often joined him and his dog on their daily walks, peeling off on the home straight and disappearing, presumably back to The Old Rectory. He said that Joker was always delightfully well behaved – how annoying!

Another chap greeted Joker like a long-lost friend. Antony had never seen this bloke before but the previous evening Joker had run off, leaving Antony up all night, worried sick when Joker didn't come home. This man, who lived over the river in one of the mill houses, said that Joker had come in through his cat flap late at night, run up the stairs and had fallen asleep on his bed – staying there until the early hours, before nipping back home, much to everyone's relief and an ear-bashing from his master.

Perhaps the funniest recent episode was when a neighbour's prized Border Terrier, Peanut, who had been mated to a Crufts-worthy compatible Adonis doggy, gave birth to a litter of fuzzy, black-and-white mini-Jokers! He had snuck his way into their supposedly Fort Knox secure property and romanced Peanut completely. She loves the rogue so much they regularly 'sing' to each other from a distance but, of course, are forbidden to see each other again, Romeo and Juliet style.

While other dogs walk to heel and come when called, and even badly behaved mutts know what their owner is saying to them and reluctantly fall into line in due course, Joker is oblivious, untrained, unruly and absolutely lovable for it. He's a quirky-looking fellow, with a strangely long body, boundless energy and, to give him some credit, he has in fact managed, albeit with some pretty exhausting, alternative therapy procedures, to get Antony back to full fighting fitness, so maybe we are all a little too hard on this rascal of a dog. Joker is perfectly named as it turns out, and it is wonderful to think that we have many more years of his derring-do to look forward to!

MATTHEW JUKES HAS WON THE IWSC TROPHY FOR COMMUNICATOR OF THE YEAR, IS THE WEEKLY WINE CORRESPONDENT FOR *THE DAILY MAIL* AND *MONEYWEEK* AND HAS BEEN VOTED THE MOST INFLUENTIAL WINE WRITER IN THE UK BY OLN. HE HAS WRITTEN THIRTEEN BEST-SELLING WINE BOOKS INCLUDING *TASTE FOOD AND WINE* (WINNER OF THE AUSTRALIAN FOOD MEDIA 'BEST FOOD AND WINE WRITING' AWARD). MATTHEW WAS AWARDED 'HONORARY AUSTRALIAN OF THE YEAR 2012' AT THE AUSTRALIA DAY FOUNDATION UK AWARDS. WWW.MATTHEWJUKES.COM

FERGUS

OWNER: ALYSON SCARBROW
FAVOURITE TOYS: TEDDY BEAR AND BALL
NAUGHTIEST DEED: UNTYING VISITORS' SHOES WHEN THEY DON'T PAY ATTENTION TO HIM
FAVOURITE FOOD: BIG BONE FROM LOCAL BUTCHERS
PET HATE: JAMIE'S RURAL FIRE SERVICE YELLOW UNIFORM
OBSESSION: BLOCKING THE CELLAR DOOR BY LYING IN FRONT OF IT

PETERSONS OF MUDGEE   MUDGEE, NSW   LABRADOODLE, 3

RUBY

OWNER: DAN BUCKLE
FAVOURITE TOY: DIRTY SOCKS
PET HATE: WASH DOWN HOSES
FAVOURITE PASTIMES: LOUNGING AROUND BETWEEN NAPS AND OCCASIONAL SCAMPERING
OBSESSION: DINNER – THE EARLIER THE BETTER
NAUGHTIEST DEED: INAPPROPRIATE USE OF HER COLD, WET SNOUT

DOMAINE CHANDON COLDSTREAM, VIC | LABRADOR, 8

CADDIE

OWNER: ELKE DAVIES
FAVOURITE TOY: ROPE TOY
PET HATE: VACUUM CLEANER
NAUGHTIEST DEED: SHOWERING ELKE'S ROOM WITH HALF-EATEN TISSUES FROM THE WASTEPAPER BASKET
FAVOURITE PASTIME: LYING ON HER BACK IN THE SUN
FAVOURITE FOODS: IRISH STEW, SPANISH CHORIZO AND CHICKEN
OBSESSION: MAKING HER DAILY ROUNDS (THAT RABBIT MIGHT STILL BE THERE)

SHEPHERDS RUN WINES AND RESTAURANT WAMBOIN, NSW | GERMAN SHORTHAIRED POINTER, 8

OWNER: PATRICK FRENCH
FAVOURITE TOY: SQUEAKY ELEPHANT
NAUGHTIEST DEEDS: WALKING IN WET CEMENT AND GETTING INTO THE CHICKEN PEN
KNOWN ACCOMPLICE: MOLLIE THE BORDER COLLIE
OBSESSION: RIDING ON GRAEME'S LAP ON THE 4-WHEELER
FAVOURITE PASTIME: CHASING PLOVERS OUT OF THE VINEYARD

TINY

AUSTRALIAN SILKY TERRIER X, 11 MONTHS | ELMSLIE WINES LEGANA, TAS

FRODO

OWNERS: JILL AND RICHARD McINTYRE
FAVOURITE PASTIME: RUNNING VERY FAST
OBSESSION: LICKING JACK THE CAT'S EARS
NAUGHTIEST DEED: CORNERING REG THE PEACOCK AND REMOVING HIS TAILFEATHERS
KNOWN ACCOMPLICES: JACK THE CAT, OSCAR AND PEDRO
PET HATES: RAIN AND GOING OUTSIDE FOR A WEE WHEN IT'S WET

MOOROODUC ESTATE MOOROODUC, VIC | STANDARD POODLE, 2

PEDRO

OWNER: KATE McINTYRE
FAVOURITE PASTIME: SLEEPING UNDER THE DOONA
FAVOURITE FOOD: VEGEMITE ON TOAST (NO CRUSTS)
FAVOURITE TOY: SOMETHING SELECTED FROM HIS TOY BOX
OBSESSION: CHECKING CORKS IN BOTTLES FOR WINE TAINT
NAUGHTIEST DEED: STOCKPILING THE OTHER DOGS' BONES
PET HATES: SCREWCAPS AND OSCAR TRYING TO BE TOP DOG

MOOROODUC ESTATE MOOROODUC, VIC | MINIATURE POODLE, 10

EVIE

OWNER: BRETT WINSLOW
OBSESSION: GARDENING AT CELLAR DOOR
KNOWN ACCOMPLICES: STELLA AND MARGARET THE CAT
PET HATES: SUDDEN MOVEMENTS AND SMALL CHILDREN
FAVOURITE TOYS: RUBBER RAT AND MARGARET THE CAT
FAVOURITE PASTIME: CHASING QUAD BIKES AND RABBITS
FAVOURITE FOOD: LEFTOVERS FROM FRIDAY AFTERNOON BBQS
NAUGHTIEST DEED: DIGGING UP THE PLANTS AT CELLAR DOOR

HEATHCOTE WINERY HEATHCOTE, VIC | KELPIE, 4

A DOG OF A WINEMAKER

by Tyson Stelzer

I'VE ALWAYS THOUGHT A DOG would make an outstanding chief winemaker.

Picture man's best friend raising a paw to give the green light to commence harvest, barking commands in the tasting room, rising majestically in his place to signal the final decision on the year's blend.

An insane suggestion? No dog can drive a tractor, prune a vine, climb a ladder to assess a ferment, connect a hose, turn on a tap. He can't even lift a glass or pick a bunch of grapes (without eating it).

But what chief winemaker ever busies themselves with such menial tasks? There's always an army of cellarhands, vineyard workers and lab techs on hand, leaving the most important decisions to, well, the top dog. And in this role our canine friend is particularly gifted.

Ask any winemaker to name their most prized asset and they will invariably point to their nose.

Meet Nick Carter. The grandfather of Bloodhound trailing folklore, Nick was born in 1900 and credited with more than 650 finds in his life, including successfully following a trail already an incredible twelve days old.

So extraordinary is the Bloodhound's sense of smell that the breed has gained fame the world over for tracking escaped prisoners, missing people, lost children and lost pets. It's sniffed out termites, drugs, explosives, guns, leaking gas pipes, bedbugs and even cancerous tumours.

Bloodhounds can track scents days later, where no tracks are visible, over great distances, even across water. They have been known to follow a human trail for more than eighty kilometres, locate bodies under water, even grave sites in flood-ravaged areas.

While you and I have some ten million olfactory receptor cells, the average dog is privileged to 200 million and a Bloodhound more than four billion. In a winery, such superhuman sensitivity could revolutionise the way wine is made.

And it already has. Miss Louisa Belle has an important responsibility at Linnaea Vineyards in Melbourne. The seven-year-old red Bloodhound ensures no cork taint contaminates a single bottle. Cork taint destroys wine, leaving it tasting like damp cardboard or even, funnily enough, wet dog. Not at Linnaea. Faced with a pile of corks, Miss Belle can isolate a tainted cork and push it aside with her snout within thirty seconds. Just a sniff of a barrel of wine will tell her whether it's off.

And, most useful of all, her owners claim she can even identify a tainted wine before the bottle is opened. Now there's a dog every wine drinker could do with!

Miss Belle is not unique. Labradors can learn that trick, too. Ziggy is a five-year-old fox-red Labrador retriever at Sojourn Cellars in Sonoma, California. So sensitive is her nose that she can detect cork taint in concentrations as low as one part per trillion. That's one-twentieth of a drop in an Olympic swimming pool.

I can see it now, packs of Bloodhounds and Labradors scouring Portuguese cork sheds with the military precision of the border protection dogs in a Heathrow arrivals hall. Had it happened years ago, the entire alternative closures industry may well have been barking up the wrong tree. In today's age of screw caps, there may seem little use for even the best cork taint detector, but higher purposes call for the superhuman sensitivity of our canine friends.

Joy is a Golden retriever who spends her days bounding along every row of Domaine Chandon's Napa Valley vineyards. She's on the hunt for something so tiny it's barely visible to the human eye, with a scent imperceptible to the human nose. Undetected, an outbreak of mealy bugs could destroy the entire crop.

After just eight weeks of training, Joy can successfully sniff out a single mealy bug scent planted in the vineyard by her trainer.

As remarkable as these stories are, there's a lot more to winemaking than simply identifying bad corks and bad vines. Is a dog even capable of recognising a good wine if one is put in front of its superhuman nose?

Louisa Belle can sniff out cork taint a mile off, but her owners admit she has no taste for wine, preferring a bowl of water and a generous helping of dog food. Could a dog even reliably recognise wine?

If any old lab rat can do it, surely our clever Bloodhounds and Labradors have a fighting chance. When Japanese researchers tested thirsty mice trained to discriminate between different liquors, they discovered that they could reliably distinguish red wine from white wine, rosé wine, sake and plum liqueur. But when it came to distinguishing cheap Japanese cask reds from Beaujolais Villages, most mice failed the test.

If a mouse can't pick one red wine from another, can a dog? And, more importantly, can it pick a dreadful one from a good one? Winemaking at its core is built on an aesthetic appreciation, an ability to identify quality fruit, the best batches and the finest blends. Surely a dog can't be trained to do that?

Or can it? The clue this time comes from a place even more unlikely than lab rats. A study that seems to all intents and purposes bird-brained, yet which earned its researchers nothing less than a Nobel prize. The premise was as simple as it was absurd: could a pigeon be trained to be an art critic?

Birds were trained to peck at a button for good paintings and do nothing in response to bad works. With never-seen works, pigeons picked good paintings twice as often as bad paintings. They successfully discriminated good from bad, watercolours from pastels, even Picasso from Monet.

If a tiny-brained pigeon can appreciate artistic excellence, surely a clever dog is capable of recognising great wine. And if it can recognise it, is there any reason it couldn't be trained to make it?

With the right conditioning, a Bloodhound, Labrador or even a little Beagle could be conditioned to roam the rows of a vineyard, munching on grapes and giving the signal to flag the start of harvest.

He could call the shots at the receival bin, sensitively nosing every batch of incoming grapes, making the decision to declassify or promote. And with the right training, why couldn't he make the call on when to take it out of oak, choose the best of the blending options and select the right time to release it to the market?

Don't be surprised when a dog's name one day appears as the chief winemaker on the back of your favourite bottle, signed with a paw print. It's about time some noble winemaker put the reins into the paws of their canine companion. With the PR they'd generate, the wine would be an instant sellout. Even if it were a dog's breakfast.

TYSON STELZER IS A MULTI-AWARD WINNING WINE WRITER WITH AN ANNUAL READERSHIP OF FOUR MILLION WORLDWIDE. HE IS THE AUTHOR AND PUBLISHER OF THIRTEEN WINE BOOKS AND A REGULAR CONTRIBUTOR TO THIRTEEN MAGAZINES.

OBSESSION: BIRDS
OWNER: MARCO PANIZZUTTI
NAUGHTIEST DEED: STEALING
PET HATE: GOING OUTSIDE IN THE COLD
FAVOURITE FOODS: PASTA AND SARDINES
FAVOURITE PASTIME: CHASING THE BIRDS
KNOWN ACCOMPLICE: BRUNO THE CANARY

SIENA

ROTTWEILER, 1 | **ST. MAUR** EXETER, NSW

DOLCE

OBSESSION: CHICKEN POOP
OWNER: TONI-MAREE BISHOP
FAVOURITE TOY: HIS HUMAN BROTHER CALLVM
FAVOURITE PASTIME: SLEEPING ON TONI-MAREE'S BED
PET HATE: LITTLE GIRLS WHO THINK HE IS A LIVE TEDDY BEAR
FAVOURITE FOOD: TURKISH BREAD STOLEN FROM LILY THE PIG

SARABAH ESTATE VINEYARD SARABAH VIA CANUNGRA, QLD | MINIATURE POODLE, 7

OWNERS: THE TONIOLO FAMILY
FAVOURITE FOOD: SCHMACKOS
FAVOURITE TOY: STUFFED PINK SPIDER
NAUGHTIEST DEED: PEEING IN THE HOUSE
KNOWN ACCOMPLICES: BILLY AND THE GIRLS
OBSESSION: ROLLING OVER AND WANTING CUDDLES
FAVOURITE PASTIME: SLEEPING ON HER BACK ON HER BEAN BAG BED

MILLIE

MALTESE X, 5 | MORNING SUN VINEYARD MAIN RIDGE, VIC

FAVOURITE FOOD: COLD PASTA
OBSESSION: ATTACKING THE GARDEN HOSE
OWNERS: CHRISTIAN AND SIMONE DAL ZOTTO
FAVOURITE PASTIME: PLAYING BOCCE AT CELLAR DOOR
PET HATES: AUNTY CARLA'S CAT AND SAUVIGNON BLANC
KNOWN ACCOMPLICES: HIS BROTHER ARNOLD AND CHARLIE THE DALMATIAN
NAUGHTIEST DEED: MAKING LIGHT WORK OF THE SALAMI HANGING IN THE WINERY

WILLIS | DAL ZOTTO WINES WHITFIELD, VIC | AUSTRALIAN BULLDOG, 5

BROOK
OWNER: JUDY GIFFORD
FAVOURITE FOOD: HMMM... BACON
NAUGHTIEST DEED: NOT COMING HOME FROM SNIFFING EXPEDITIONS
FAVOURITE TOY: THE CAT'S SQUEAKY BALL
FAVOURITE PASTIME: FOLLOWING KODY AROUND
PET HATE: BEING PEED ON BY HIS TALLER BROTHER
OBSESSIONS: CHASING THE CAT AND PEEING ON EVERYTHING

KODY
PET HATE: THE BATH
OWNER: JUDY GIFFORD
FAVOURITE FOOD: CHICKEN
FAVOURITE TOY: HIS BRO BROOK
NAUGHTIEST DEED: PEEING ON EVERYTHING
OBSESSION: MARKING THE NEIGHBOURHOOD
FAVOURITE PASTIME: ROMPING WITH HIS BRO

TOY POODLES, 4 | DARLING PARK WINERY RED HILL, VIC

DOUGLAS

PET HATE: DEEP WATER
FAVOURITE TOY: TEDDY BEAR
OWNERS: THE McNALLY FAMILY
OBSESSIONS: RABBITS AND BALLS
FAVOURITE PASTIMES: SLEEPING AND MEET 'N' GREET
NAUGHTIEST DEED: RUNNING AWAY WITH BEST FRIEND KRYTEN

JASPER HILL VINEYARD HEATHCOTE, VIC | GERMAN SHORTHAIRED POINTER, 10

KNOWN ACCOMPLICE: BOSS
OWNERS: GINA AND LEO PALAZZO
PET HATE: HAVING HIS TAIL BRUSHED
OBSESSION: FINDING MUDDY PUDDLES
FAVOURITE PASTIME: STIRRING UP THE HORSES
FAVOURITE FOOD: KILLARA ESTATE'S FAMOUS LASAGNE
NAUGHTIEST DEED: EATING A WEEK'S SUPPLY OF SAUSAGES

WINSTON

SAINT BERNARD, 3 | **KILLARA ESTATE** SEVILLE EAST, VIC

BARNEY

OWNER: PASCALE LATRAS
PET HATE: KOOKABURRAS
FAVOURITE TOY: SOCCER BALL
OBSESSION: PLAYING SOCCER WITH CHILDREN
KNOWN ACCOMPLICE: JEZZA THE VINEYARD CAT
NAUGHTIEST DEED: STEALING THE CHOOKS' FOOD
FAVOURITE PASTIME: GREETING CUSTOMERS AT CELLAR DOOR

MRS NICKS VINEYARD BALNARRING, VIC | BORDER COLLIE, 2

JOEY
NAUGHTIEST DEED: EATING OFF THE TABLE (EGGED ON BY MAX)
FAVOURITE FOOD: CHICKEN NECKS
OWNERS: MAREE COLLIS AND RAY NADESON
FAVOURITE PASTIME: SITTING ON THE COUCH
FAVOURITE TOY: BABY'S TOY THAT HE ARRIVED WITH

MAX
FAVOURITE PASTIME: ESCAPING
PET HATE: BEING LOCKED OUTSIDE
OWNERS: MAREE COLLIS AND RAY NADESON
NAUGHTIEST DEED: EATING HALF A KILO OF CALLEBAUT CHOCOLATE AND NEEDING TO HAVE HIS STOMACH PUMPED
FAVOURITE TOY: RARE BREED OF DUCK THAT RESIDES NEXT DOOR

HARRY

OBSESSION: THE CAT
NAUGHTIEST DEED: PASSING WIND AT HIGHLY INAPPROPRIATE TIMES
FAVOURITE FOOD: VEGEMITE ON TOAST
PET HATE: BEING EVICTED FROM THE COUCH
OWNERS: TIM ADAMS AND PAM GOLDSACK
FAVOURITE PASTIMES: HOGGING THE COUCH AND ROLLING IN UNMENTIONABLE THINGS

SAM

PET HATE: BATH TIME
FAVOURITE PASTIME: PLAYING UNDER THE SPRINKLERS
FAVOURITE TOY: STOLEN UGG BOOTS
NAUGHTIEST DEED: DEMOLISHING A BRAND NEW PAIR OF NIKE SNEAKERS
OWNERS: TIM ADAMS AND PAM GOLDSACK

TIM ADAMS WINES CLARE, SA | GROODLES, 2

OWNER: KARINA KROEHN
PET HATE: AN EMPTY BOWL
FAVOURITE FOOD: PIGS EARS
KNOWN ACCOMPLICES: OLLIE AND JAZZ
NAUGHTIEST DEED: TAKING THE 5KM TREK FROM HOME TO THE EDEN VALLEY PUB
FAVOURITE PASTIME: HELPING TO BRING IN THE SHEEP
FAVOURITE TOY: THE COOPERS STOUT BRASS MONKEY DOLL

PIPPA

GOLDEN RETRIEVER, 5 MONTHS | TASTE EDEN VALLEY REGIONAL WINE ROOM ANGASTON, SA

PATTERSON

OBSESSION: BRIONI
FAVOURITE FOOD: PIZZA FROM THE WOOD OVEN AT CELLAR DOOR
OWNER: BRIONI OLIVER
FAVOURITE PASTIME: RIDING IN THE BACK OF BRIONI'S UTE
FAVOURITE TOY: THE WAVES AT MOANA BEACH
PET HATES: COURIERS AND WHEELIE BIN TYRES
NAUGHTIEST DEED: PESTERING CELLAR DOOR VISITORS FOR A PAT

OLIVER'S TARANGA McLAREN VALE, SA | RHODESIAN RIDGEBACK X, 8

FAVOURITE TOY: MISS PIGGY
OWNERS: THE BROWN FAMILY
FAVOURITE FOOD: THE NEXT MEAL
OBSESSION: HUMPING HIS BLANKET
PET HATE: THE THOUGHT OF SLEEPING OUTSIDE
NAUGHTIEST DEED: EATING DYNAMIC LIFTER FROM THE GARDEN
FAVOURITE PASTIME: STEALING ATTENTION FROM HIS OLDER SISTERS

OWNER: WILLY LUNN
FAVOURITE TOY: STICKS
OBSESSION: WATER HOSES
KNOWN ACCOMPLICES: MILLY AND LULU
FAVOURITE FOOD: MEAT, MEAT AND MEAT
PET HATE: NOT BEING ABLE TO COME INTO WORK
FAVOURITE PASTIMES: SWIMMING AND SLEEPING
NAUGHTIEST DEEDS: FARTING AND COMING HOME COVERED IN MUD

YERING STATION YARRA GLEN, VIC | LABRADOR, 2

THE AUTOBIOGRAPHY OF
FLING FORRESTAL

by Peter Forrestal

YOU MIGHT WONDER WHY A HUNGRY BEAGLE LIKE ME would be putting pen to paper (actually 'paw to keyboard') to dash off this autobiography. Fair call. Well, I come from a family of writers, so why should I be the odd one out. The alpha male, Forrie, is a wine writer and writes non-fiction so you can't believe a thing he says, while my mother-figure, Elaine, writes fiction and so everything she writes is the truth.

You might find it a bit strange but in a quasi-literary family like this a beagle picks up a fair whack. There are several key influences on this autobiography of mine. Firstly, Gertrude Stein's Autobiography of Alice B. Toklas. Now, unlike the rest of the family, I've never been to Paris – I used to get sent back to my breeders when they whizzed off but now I go to the grandchildren's. I've picked up lots about Paris from the Gertrude Stein book and plenty about her but nothing much about Alice B. Toklas – it's that kind of autobiography. Then there's the Russian poet, Vevgeny Yevtushenko, who was 30 when he wrote his A Precocious Autobiography. I'm about the same age (in dog years) as Yevtushenko was when he wrote his book, and so it seems timely for me to write my first autobiography. Certainly, the most important influence on my writing is the American poet, Don Marquis, and the books he wrote exploiting the poetry of the cockroach, Archy (in Archy and Mehitabel). Google 'the coming of Archy' to find out how Archy got started as a poet. I figured that if a cockroach could write poetry then a beagle could write an autobiography.

I know what you want to know: I was born on 10th April 2004 at Sligrachan Kennels on the edge of the Swan Valley – my father was Angus and my mother Goldie and I was one of a litter of four. Forget all that. What you do need to know about was my first con job or sting. When he's starting out in life, a beagle needs a family and a comfortable place to live (preferably a sourdough producing bakery). You can't rely solely on puppy cuteness so I decided on a strategy to get noticed. I positioned myself on the edge of the litter, furthest from Goldie (except for a quick dash to the nipple for milk).

My breeders, Marion and the late Joe Watson, knew that the Forrestals needed a beagle pup and so took a photo of our litter on the day after we were born. There I was, the independent one, on the edge. I had an extensive jet black saddle at birth but was much more of a tricolour beagle by week four when the Forrestals came to decide on which pup they would choose. It just needed a little sleight of paw when our visitors arrived to stand out from the crowd. 'Pick me! Pick me!' I grinned as I drifted over to the edge of the cage. When they fell for that and picked me up, it was all over bar the shouting. I had all the tricks covered: the gentle lick of the chin, the snuggle into the arm, the limp flop into the arms. Then there was the wait until I was 12 weeks old and could take up residence in my family home. I wasn't going to mention this but I did throw up in the car on the way home – three times.

One of the great luxuries of writing an autobiography is that you get to refute some of the more scurrilous accusations made against you in earlier times. I'm still deeply hurt by some of the comments made about me in an earlier edition of Wine Dogs Australia *(A good book, but there's some dodgy commentary there.) To describe an energetic young pup as 'manic' seems callous, even hurtful. And while there's a hint of accuracy in the description of some of the personal items that I'm accused of destroying, the circumstances are never fully explained. I was performing a kindly service to the family when I removed the carpet from its customary position – it was way past its best, in need of urgent replacement – and they just chose not to see that. Similarly, with any furniture that I helped consign to the annual rubbish collection. And the items of a personal nature: well, he was going way over his limit on those credit cards, needed more stylish jumpers (pullovers, well really, hasn't anyone told him?), and used the mobile phone far too often... Surely, you understand.*

As beagles go, I'm a home body. There's plenty of space outdoors on the Cobb Street corner block, heaps of shade from trees – two olive trees (kalamatas) planted in 1961 – and a lilly pilly tree with its edible berries. And it's only 400 metres to the dog beach. One of the great things about being a home body is visitors. As a wine writer's beagle, there are several couriers each day who call in to see me and leave samples. Then there are the wine tastings – usually three times a week – when the panel chairman comes along to give me a long luxurious pat, and then lets me in and out of the front door several times during the tasting. My most important job at the tasting is looking out for JJ. I have a seat overlooking the window, and after the others have arrived, I sit quietly until I see JJ arrive. Then I let them know that JJ is late. They don't seem surprised. It's quite demanding being a wine writer's dog.

Then there are the grandchildren. Every dog should have grandchildren. They are just the right height – for a pat or a cuddle, or when they have some food, to mug them. I have two grandchildren, Issac (5) who's called 'Digger' by his sister, Naomi, who is two. Frankly, Issac is getting a bit old and he's more difficult to mug than he used to be but Naomi is just right. She has learned to defend herself pretty well but it's better than having to deal with adults all the time. With them you have to look cute – and famished. But it doesn't work very often.

I'd been reading about protection rackets and decided to introduce the Schmackos trick. They want to leave the house, I get a Schmacko. They're not sure if I'm charging a toll for them leaving the house or demanding a payment for looking after the house while they're gone. You leave, I get a Schmacko, no one gets hurt. When they return, I feign disinterest.

It's not a bad life for a beagle, sharing a house with two writers but I do get pretty hungry.

BEAGLE FANCIER, **PETER FORRESTAL**, IS A FREELANCE WINE WRITER BASED IN PERTH WHO WRITES FOR NATIONAL AND INTERNATIONAL PUBLICATIONS INCLUDING *GOURMET TRAVELLER WINE*, *QANTAS MAGAZINE* AND *MONEY MAGAZINE*. HE IS WORKING ON RELEASING HIS GUIDE TO BUDGET-PRICED WINES, *QUAFF*, AS AN APP. HE WAS FOUNDING EDITOR OF *GOURMET TRAVELLER WINE* AND HIS 33 BOOKS INCLUDE THE *GLOBAL ENCYCLOPAEDIA OF WINE*.

LOLA

FAVOURITE TOY: BUNGS
OWNER: KATE PETERING
FAVOURITE FOOD: GIANT BONES
NAUGHTIEST DEED: ANKLE BITING
KNOWN ACCOMPLICES: KP, AZZA AND WELLY
FAVOURITE PASTIME: BASKING IN THE WARMTH OF THE OFFICE
PET HATES: COLD MORNINGS, WATER HOSES AND BEING LEFT BEHIND
OBSESSION: DIGGING UNDERNEATH ANYTHING IN SEARCH OF THE PERFECT RABBIT

MOUNT LANGI GHIRAN BAYINDEEN, VIC | TERRIER X, 3

OWNERS: THE WHISH-WILSON FAMILY
NAUGHTIEST DEEDS: DIGGING UP YOUNG VINES AND ROLLING ON SMELLY THINGS
KNOWN ACCOMPLICES: ELVIS PRETZEL AND DARCY
FAVOURITE FOODS: FLIES AND GINGERBREAD MEN
PET HATES: DESIGNER DOGS AND TOURISTS WHO DON'T BUY WINE
FAVOURITE PASTIMES: CHASING SEAGULLS AND SLEEPING ON BEDS
OBSESSIONS: BROOMS, VACUUM CLEANERS AND EXPENSIVE SUNGLASSES

DIVA

STAFFORDSHIRE TERRIER X, 7 | **THREE WISHES VINEYARD** HILLWOOD, TAS

FLEUR
OBSESSION: BALLS
PET HATE: BEING LEFT ALONE
FAVOURITE FOOD: SCHMACKOS
NAUGHTIEST DEED: PUTTING RAW BONES IN VISITORS' SUITCASES
OWNERS: PETER AND ANN WORMALD
FAVOURITE PASTIME: BARKING AT THE HORSES

AIMEE
OBSESSION: BALLS
FAVOURITE TOY: BLANKETS
FAVOURITE FOOD: SCHMACKOS
OWNERS: PETER AND ANN WORMALD
NAUGHTIEST DEED: PUTTING CHICKEN WINGS BETWEEN THE PILLOWS
FAVOURITE PASTIME: GREETING VISITORS

THE WILLOW LANE VINEYARD MUDGEE, NSW | MINIATURE POODLES, 10 & 3

FAVOURITE TOY: DASH'S BOOTS
OWNERS: DARREN AND SUZ WESTLAKE
FAVOURITE PASTIME: CHASING THE CATS
OBSESSION: LOOKING THROUGH WINDOWS (INCLUDING THE NEIGHBOUR'S)
NAUGHTIEST DEED: HIDING DASH'S BOOTS OUT IN THE RAIN
KNOWN ACCOMPLICES: OTTO THE CAT AND DOLLY THE SHEEP

EDDIE

BERNESE MOUNTAIN DOG, 1 | **WESTLAKE VINEYARDS** KOONUNGA, SA

MURPHY BROWN

OWNER: SAMANTHA CONNEW
FAVOURITE TOY: FLETCHER THE CAT
KNOWN ACCOMPLICES: SHIM AND ROSIE
OBSESSIONS: SQUEEGEES, WATER HOSES AND BROOMS
FAVOURITE PASTIMES: EATING AND RUNNING WITH SAM
PET HATE: VANESSA THE DOG GROOMER BLOW-DRYING HER EARS
NAUGHTIEST DEED: DEVOURING 16 MINI CHRISTMAS PUDDINGS AND THEN BARFING THEM UP ON THE McLAREN VALE RUNNING TRACK

PETRICHOR WINE CO. POKOLBIN, NSW | LABRADOR, 7

PET HATE: BATH TIME
OWNERS: TONY AND DEBBIE McKENDRY
FAVOURITE PASTIME: WELCOMING CUSTOMERS
NAUGHTIEST DEED: CHEWING A COMPUTER CORD
FAVOURITE TOY: AN OLD TOWELLING SURF BOARD
OBSESSION: PLASTIC CONTAINERS LEFT AROUND THE YARD

RAFFA

JACK RUSSELL TERRIER X, 1 | **VINIFERA WINES** MUDGEE, NSW

BOB

OBSESSION: SHOES
FAVOURITE TOY: SHOES
FAVOURITE PASTIME: CHASING WHISKERS
OWNERS: DARREN HAUNOLD AND FAMILY
NAUGHTIEST DEED: EATING THE VINEYARD HANDS' LUNCHES WHILE THEY ARE PICKING AND PRUNING
KNOWN ACCOMPLICES: RUSSELL AND WHISKERS

WILLS DOMAIN YALLINGUP, WA | BORDER COLLIE, 8 MONTHS

FAVOURITE TOY: TEDDY
OBSESSIONS: FOOD AND SLEEP
OWNERS: PAUL BRIDGEMAN AND CAROLINE MOONEY
FAVOURITE PASTIME: RIDING IN THE DRIVER'S SEAT IN THE UTE
PET HATES: COLD MORNINGS AND HAVING HIS SLEEP DISTURBED
NAUGHTIEST DEED: POOING IN THE TASTING ROOM BEFORE A VIP VISIT
FAVOURITE FOOD: ANYTHING STOLEN FROM GRAPE PICKERS' BACKPACKS

ARCHIE

JACK RUSSELL TERRIER, 4   YARRA YERING GRUYERE, VIC

JEEPERS

PET HATE: BATHS
OBSESSION: THINGS BEING THROWN
OWNERS: MARK AND VIKKI MESSENGER
FAVOURITE PASTIME: LEADING PEOPLE ON A BIKE RIDE ON THE 'RAILS TO TRAILS' TRACK
NAUGHTIEST DEED: CROSSING A BUSY ROAD TO VISIT WORKERS HAVING MORNING TEA
FAVOURITE TOYS: HONKEY NUTS, BALLS AND BARK CHIPS

JUNIPER ESTATE COWARAMUP, WA | KELPIE X, 11

"Some of our greatest historical and artistic treasures we place with curators in museums; others we take for walks."

—— **ROGER CARAS**

MISSY
PET HATE: VISITING THE VET
FAVOURITE FOOD: ANYTHING IN HARRY'S BOWL, FOLLOWED BY HERS
OBSESSION: DUMPING DEAD ANIMAL REMAINS ON THE FRONT DOORSTEP
OWNERS: STEPHEN AND LEANNE WEBBER
NAUGHTIEST DEED: CONSTANTLY DUMPING DEAD ANIMAL REMAINS ON THE FRONT DOORSTEP

HARRY
PET HATE: THE CAT
OWNERS: STEPHEN AND LEANNE WEBBER
FAVOURITE PASTIMES: SLEEPING AND EATING
FAVOURITE FOODS: LEFTOVER STEAK AND PIZZA
NAUGHTIEST DEED: EATING A DUCK FROM OFF THE BBQ
OBSESSION: OFFERING PEOPLE LEAVES IN EXCHANGE FOR FOOD

LABRADORS, 8 & 12 | **DE BORTOLI WINES** DIXONS CREEK, VIC

WHAT'S IN A NAME..?

by Craig McGill

IT MAY SEEM ODD that our latest Wine Dogs Australia 3 book is in fact the fifth Australian edition and the tenth in the Wine Dogs international series overall but I'll attempt to explain the series of events that led to our strange numbering system. In 2003 when the first Wine Dogs book was published we had no idea of the phenomenon that we'd created. There were no plans for a second book, even when the first print run sold out in a matter of months. Then we were inundated with requests from wineries that missed the first call for entries but also wanted their dogs to bathe in the glory, so the reprint was expanded to accommodate the new dogs and we called it Wine Dogs Deluxe. *But we still underestimated how popular this little book was until we were swamped with entries from wineries all around the world. Wine Dogs had gone from a pet project we did for a bit of fun into a potential global publishing empire. We couldn't name every book* Wine Dogs, *even if they were in different parts of the world, so we decided to add a country name to each title. This is how* Wine Dogs Australia *became the third Australian edition and so on....*

Talk about little things that can change the course of your life, Wine Dogs is one such story that has changed our lives in many ways. I think the most significant lesson is teaching us to follow our passions. Job satisfaction has got to be the main motivation in anything we pursue. If it's not fun, don't do it. Easier said than done, I remind myself, after a mischievous hound pees on my camera bag or worse still, my leg! Or I pick up a gorgeous-looking pooch only to discover that they have been for a roll in something that's been dead for three weeks ... and they look at you as if to say "oh don't you love me anymore?" with their manipulative sad eyes. But we don't dare complain, as I know how blessed we are to travel the world, eating and drinking our way through the seemingly infinite number of wineries and playing with the dogs that share these great wine estates of the world. It's sheer indulgence and we love it.

So what do we call the next book? Who cares, let's just pack the bags and go... we have 38,000 more wineries to visit.

STATS, FACTS & WOOFILEAKS...

by Craig McGill

WE OFTEN GET ASKED QUESTIONS about the production of our books. Some are easy to answer and some require a more diplomatic response. "Is Fluffy the smartest dog you've ever met?" or "Will Howard be on the cover?" usually tests our ability to keep a straight face but it's hard when our job is so much fun... after all, aren't they all cover worthy? We never 'out' any of the more difficult hounds or owners and all names have been changed to protect the innocent. Here are some of the 'facts' relating to the production of Wine Dogs Australia 3:

- *Number of days of photography: 68*
- *Kilometres travelled by car: 5,433*
- *Kilometres travelled by plane: 14,846*
- *Number of States and Territories visited: 8 (ACT, New South Wales, Northern Territory, Queensland, South Australia twice, Tasmania, Victoria twice and Western Australia three times)*
- *Number of Northern Territory Wine Dogs: nil*
- *Number of times we got lost: nil*
- *Number of wrong turns: &*%$#*!!!*
- *Amount of destroyed clothing: 3 shirts, 2 shoelaces*
- *Most common dog breed: Labrador (24)*
- *Least common breed: Eight-legged spider terrier (nil)*
- *Number of wineries featured in this edition: 150*
- *Total number of dogs photographed for this edition: 235*
- *Number of wineries visited worldwide by Wine Dogs: 1,886 (as of July 2012)*
- *Number of dogs referred to by the owner as 'gifted' or a 'genius': 4*
- *Number of dogs that couldn't sit when asked: 86*
- *Number of pedigree dogs: 37*
- *Number of rescue dogs: 88*
- *Number of kangaroos photographed: 1*
- *Number of pigs photographed: 1*
- *Number of dogs with their own Twitter account: 5*
- *Number of pigs with their own Twitter account: 1*

- Number of dogs with their own Facebook account: 4
- Number of times the photographer was bitten by a dog: nil
- Number of times the photographer was bitten by the owner: 2
- Number of times the photographer bit the dog: 1
- Most common dog names: Max (5) and Molly (4)
- Number of dogs named after grape varieties: 1
- Number of bottles of wine gifted by generous wineries: 165
- Number of wines tasted: 433
- Number of dogs with lingerie fetishes: 4
- Number of dogs that drink wine or eat grapes (not recommended for health reasons): 43
- Favourite restaurant: Sepia Restaurant, Sydney NSW
- Favourite brewpub: Murray's Craft Brewing Co., Port Stephens NSW
- Favourite meat pie: Parker Pies, Rutherglen VIC
- Favourite pizza: Giant Steps Innocent Bystander Winery, Healesville VIC
- Favourite wine bar: The Dispensary Enoteca, Bendigo VIC
- Favourite lunch restaurant: The Rockford Stonewall Table, Barossa Valley SA
- Favourite café: Breakfast and Beer, Daylesford VIC
- Favourite coffee shop: The Final Step Coffee Shop, South Yarra VIC
- Most original dog name: Nick Stock's Frenchie, Ricky Bobby
- Number of dogs that have their own business cards: 3
- Number of dogs that have eaten furniture or electrical appliances: 5
- Number of dogs 'turned on' by being photographed: 23

PHOTOGRAPHY

Craig with Bones from Keever Vineyards, Yountville, California USA

PHOTOGRAPHY © CRAIG McGILL 2012

SUSAN ELLIOTT

SYDNEY, NSW

SUSAN IS A MULTI-SKILLED ARTIST WITH A BACKGROUND IN FINE ART, ILLUSTRATION AND PRINTMAKING. AFTER COMPLETING TWO YEARS OF A PSYCHOLOGY DEGREE, SUE CHANGED TO A CAREER IN ART. SHE GRADUATED FROM THE CITY ART INSTITUTE IN 1986, MAJORING IN DRAWING, PRINTMAKING AND PAINTING.

AFTER TWO YEARS LIVING ABROAD, SUE RETURNED TO AUSTRALIA AND EXHIBITED HER GRAPHIC ART AND SCREENPRINTS EXTENSIVELY AROUND SYDNEY, WHILE ALSO WORKING IN A NUMBER OF SMALL DESIGN STUDIOS. SHE HAS DEVELOPED INTO AN AWARD-WINNING GRAPHIC DESIGNER WITH OVER 20 YEARS OF EXPERIENCE IN THE INDUSTRY.

SUE JOINED McGILL DESIGN GROUP IN 1999 AS CO-OWNER AND CREATIVE DIRECTOR. SHE IS ALSO CO-FOUNDER AND PRINCIPAL OF THE GIANT DOG PUBLISHING HOUSE, WHICH IS RESPONSIBLE FOR PRODUCING A NUMBER OF BEST-SELLING BOOKS, INCLUDING THE WINE DOGS TITLES.

Stella and Sue

FAVOURITE FOOD: NOODLES
FAVOURITE PASTIME: WATCHING '70s AUSTRALIAN FILMS
KNOWN ACCOMPLICES: THE CLOWN LOACHES
OBSESSIONS: BATH SALTS AND CRYPTIC CROSSWORDS
PET HATES: WHISTLING AND RAISIN TOAST WITH PEEL

SUE'S KNOWLEDGE OF DOGS IS UNPARALLELED, AND IN THE PAST SHE HAS ALSO FOUND TIME TO BE A SUCCESSFUL SIBERIAN HUSKY BREEDER. ALTHOUGH CURRENTLY DOGLESS, SUE LOVES TO SPEND TIME WITH THE MANY WINE DOGS SHE MEETS FROM AROUND THE WORLD. SUE IS A LOVER OF WINE AND USUALLY REACHES FOR HER FAVORITE RIESLING OR PINOT NOIR WHEN FEELING A LITTLE HUSKY.

GIANT DOG PUBLISHING

GIANT DOG IS A NICHE INDEPENDENT PUBLISHING HOUSE SPECIALISING IN PRODUCING BENCHMARK QUALITY DESIGN AND ART BOOKS. RECENT PUBLICATIONS INCLUDE *WINE DOGS USA* 3, *WINE DOGS AUSTRALIA* 3, *WINE DOGS ITALY*, *WINE DOGS NEW ZEALAND* AND *FOOTY DOGS*.
www.giantdog.com.au

CRAIG McGILL

SYDNEY, NSW

ORIGINALLY FROM SHEPPARTON, VICTORIA, CRAIG IS A SELF-TAUGHT DESIGNER AND ILLUSTRATOR WHO STARTED HIS OWN DESIGN BUSINESS IN MELBOURNE AT 18 YEARS OF AGE. DURING THAT TIME HE WAS APPOINTED AS A DESIGN CONSULTANT TO THE RESERVE BANK OF AUSTRALIA.

HIS DESIGNS AND ILLUSTRATIONS HAVE GRACED BANKNOTES THROUGHOUT THE WORLD, INCLUDING THE AUSTRALIAN BICENTENARY TEN-DOLLAR NOTE. HIS WORK APPEARS ON THE ORIGINAL AUSTRALIAN $100 NOTE, PAPUA NEW GUINEA KINA, COOK ISLAND DOLLARS AND ENGLISH POUND TRAVELLER'S CHEQUES. CRAIG WAS ALSO INVOLVED IN THE DESIGN AND ILLUSTRATION OF MANY COUNTRIES' SECURITY DOCUMENTS SUCH AS PASSPORTS, BONDS AND TRAVELLER'S CHEQUES.

AT THE AGE OF 23 HE DESIGNED THE ENTIRE SERIES OF THE COOK ISLAND BANKNOTES AND IT IS BELIEVED THAT HE WAS THE WORLD'S YOUNGEST DESIGNER TO DESIGN A COUNTRY'S COMPLETE CURRENCY. IN 1991, CRAIG MOVED TO SYDNEY WHERE HIS ILLUSTRATIONS WERE REGULARLY COMMISSIONED BY AGENCIES AND DESIGNERS BOTH IN AUSTRALIA AND AROUND THE WORLD.

Craig and Tarka

DATE OF BIRTH: DEAD IN DOG YEARS
FAVOURITE FOOD: ROAST DUCK AND PINOT NOIR
FAVOURITE PASTIMES: VENTRILOQUISM AND BEING A BIG KID
NAUGHTIEST DEED: CHASING HUSKIES WHILE STARK NAKED
OBSESSIONS: BEER, WINE AND COLLECTING USELESS THINGS
KNOWN ACCOMPLICES: THE VOICES IN MY HEAD
PET HATE: UNORIGINAL IDEAS

HE IS NOW WIDELY KNOWN AS AUSTRALIA'S ONLY FREELANCE CURRENCY DESIGNER. CRAIG HAS ALSO DESIGNED AND ILLUSTRATED NINE STAMPS FOR AUSTRALIA POST.

CRAIG HAS BEEN CREATIVE DIRECTOR OF HIS OWN AGENCY, McGILL DESIGN GROUP, FOR OVER TWENTY-FIVE YEARS.

HAVING GROWN UP WITH A SUCCESSION OF BEAGLES AND HUSKIES, CRAIG IS CURRENTLY ROAD-TESTING SEVERAL HUNDRED DOG BREEDS FROM WINERIES AROUND THE WORLD. www.realnasty.com.au

McGILL DESIGN GROUP

McGILL DESIGN GROUP WAS FORMED IN 1981 AND SPECIALISES IN PROVIDING A WIDE RANGE OF QUALITY GRAPHIC DESIGN SERVICES. THE STUDIO HAS PRODUCED NUMEROUS FINE WINE LABELS AND PACKAGING AS WELL AS CORPORATE IDENTITIES, ADVERTISING, PUBLICATIONS AND TELEVISION COMMERCIALS. www.mcgilldesigngroup.com

WINERY AND VINEYARD LISTINGS

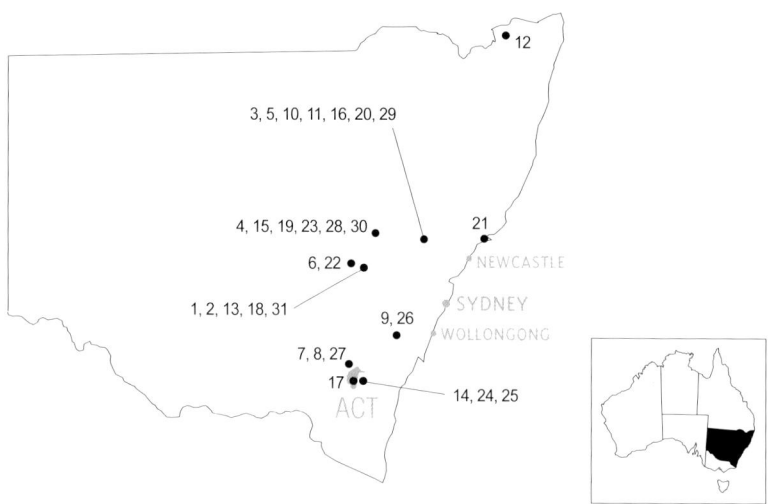

AUSTRALIAN CAPITAL TERRITORY AND NEW SOUTH WALES

1. **Belgravia Wines** PAGE 80
   Belgravia Rd, Orange NSW 2800
   Ph: (02) 6360 0495
   www.belgravia.com.au

2. **Brangayne of Orange** PAGE 60
   837 Pinnacle Rd, Orange NSW 2800
   Ph: (02) 6365 3229
   www.brangayne.com

3. **Brokenwood Wines** PAGES 46, 47
   McDonalds Rd, Pokolbin NSW 2320
   Ph: (02) 4998 7559
   www.brokenwood.com.au

4. **Bunnamagoo Wines** PAGE 59
   603 Henry Lawson Drive,
   Mudgee NSW 2850
   Ph: (02) 6373 3046
   www.bunnamagoowines.com.au

5. **Charteris Wine Company** PAGES 94, 95
   PO Box 800, Cessnock NSW 2325
   Ph: (02) 4998 7701
   www.charteriswines.com

6. **Cumulus Estate Wines** PAGE 82
   1705 Euchareena Rd, Molong NSW 2866
   Ph: (02) 6390 7900
   www.cumuluswines.com.au

7. **Dionysus Winery** PAGE 35
   1 Patemans Lane,
   Murrumbateman NSW 2582
   Ph: (02) 6227 0208
   www.dionysus-winery.com.au

8. **Eden Road Wines** PAGES 22, 23
   3182 Barton Highway,
   Murrumbateman NSW 2582
   Ph: (02) 6226 8800
   www.edenroadwines.com.au

9. **Eling Forest Winery** PAGE 63
   12587 Hume Hwy,
   Sutton Forest NSW 2577
   Ph: (02) 4878 9155
   www.elingforest.com.au

10. **Genesis Vineyard
    and Farmhouse** PAGE 62
    483 Talga Rd, Rothbury NSW 2320
    Ph: 0402 426 771
    www.genesisvineyard.com.au

11. **Gundog Estate** PAGE 103
    101 McDonalds Rd, Pokolbin NSW 2320
    Ph: (02) 4998 6873
    www.gundogestate.com.au

12. **Ilnam Estate** PAGE 107
    750 Carool Rd, Carool NSW 2486
    Ph: (07) 5590 7703
    www.ilnam.com.au

13. **La Colline** PAGE 191
    42 Lake Canobolas Rd,
    Orange NSW 2800
    Ph: (02) 6365 3275
    www.racinerestaurant.com.au

14. **Lerida Estate** PAGES 54, 55
    Old Federal Hwy,
    Lake George NSW 2581
    Ph: (02) 4848 0231
    www.leridaestate.com.au

15. **Logan Wines** PAGE 169
    1320 Castlereagh Hwy,
    Apple Tree Flat, Mudgee NSW 2850
    Ph: (02) 6373 1333
    www.loganwines.com.au

16. **Marsh Estate** PAGE 112
    Deasys Rd, Pokolbin NSW 2320
    Ph: (02) 4998 7587
    www.marshestate.com.au

17. **Mount Majura Vineyard** PAGE 204
    RMB 314 Majura Rd,
    Majura ACT 2609
    Ph: (02) 6262 3070
    www.mountmajura.com.au

18. **Patina Wines** PAGE 183
    109 Summerhill Lane,
    Orange NSW 2800
    Ph: (02) 6362 8336
    www.patinawines.com.au

19. **Petersons of Mudgee** PAGE 182
    Lot 6, Blacksprings Rd,
    Mudgee NSW 2850
    Ph: (02) 6373 3184
    www.petersonswines.com.au

20. **Petrichor Wine Co.** PAGE 224
    699 McDonalds Rd, Pokolbin NSW 2320
    Ph: 0408 173 335
    www.petrichor.com.au

21. **Port Stephens Winery** PAGE 151
    3443 Nelson Bay Rd,
    Bobs Farm NSW 2316
    Ph: (02) 4982 6411
    www.murraysbrewingco.com.au

22. **Printhie Wines** PAGE 171
    489 Yuranigh Rd, Molong NSW 2866
    Ph: (02) 6366 8422
    www.printhiewines.com.au

23. **Robert Stein Winery** PAGE 68
    Pipeclay Lane, Mudgee NSW 2850
    Ph: (02) 6373 3991
    www.robertstein.com.au

24. **Shaw Vineyard Estate** PAGE 167
    34 Isabel Drive,
    Murrumbateman NSW 2582
    Ph: (02) 6227 5827
    www.shawvineyards.com.au

25. **Shepherds Run Wines
    and Restaurant** PAGE 186
    344 Norton Rd, Wamboin NSW 2620
    Ph: (02) 6238 3842
    www.shepherdsrun.com.au

26. **St. Maur** PAGE 197
    Old Argyle Rd, Exeter NSW 2579
    Ph: (02) 4883 4401
    www.stmaurwines.com.au

27. **Tallagandra Hill** PAGE 229
    1692 Murrumbateman Rd,
    Gundaroo NSW 2620
    Ph: (02) 6236 8694
    www.tallagandrahill.com.au

28. **The Willow Lane Vineyard** PAGE 222
    161 Eurunderee Lane,
    Mudgee NSW 2850
    Ph: (02) 6373 3131
    www.thewillowlane.com.au

29. **Tower Estate** PAGE 21
    Halls Rd, Pokolbin NSW 2320
    Ph: (02) 4998 7989
    www.towerestate.com

30. **Vinifera Wines** PAGE 225
    194 Henry Lawson Drive,
    Mudgee NSW 2850
    Ph: (02) 6372 2461
    www.viniferawines.com.au

31. **Word of Mouth Wines** PAGE 166
    790 Pinnacle Rd, Orange NSW 2800
    Ph: (02) 6365 3509
    www.wordofmouthwines.com.au

QUEENSLAND

1. **Jester Hill Wines** PAGE 108
   292 Mt Stirling Rd,
   Glen Aplin QLD 4381
   Ph: (07) 4683 4380
   www.jesterhillwines.com.au

2. **Sarabah Estate Vineyard** PAGE 198
   46 Rymera Rd, Sarabah via
   Canungra QLD 4275
   Ph: (07) 5543 4746
   www.sarabahestate.com.au

SOUTH AUSTRALIA

1. **Balnaves of Coonawarra** PAGE 24
   Riddoch Hwy, Coonawarra SA 5263
   Ph: (08) 8737 2946
   www.balnaves.com.au

2. **Barratt Wines** PAGE 75
   2 Cornish Rd, Summertown SA 5141
   Ph: (08) 8390 1788
   www.barrattwines.com.au

3. **Barristers Block Wines** PAGE 78
   141 Onkaparinga Valley Rd,
   Woodside SA 5244
   Ph: (08) 8389 7706
   www.barristersblock.com.au

4. **Bellwether Wines** PAGE 86
   Glen Roy Shearing Shed,
   Riddoch Hwy, Coonawarra SA 5263
   Ph: 0417 080 945
   www.bellwetherwines.com.au

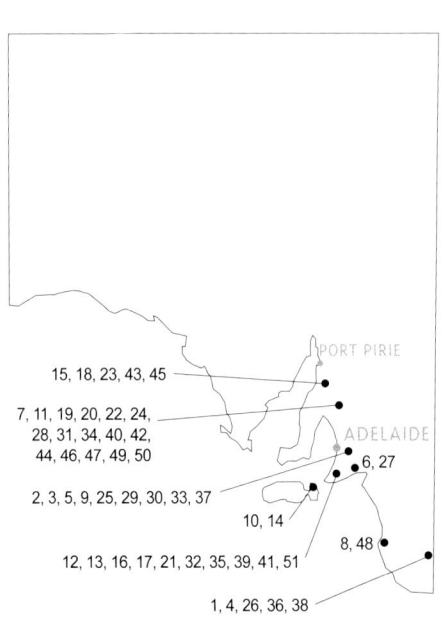

WINERY AND VINEYARD LISTINGS: SOUTH AUSTRALIA

5. **Bird in Hand** PAGES 37, 253
   150 Pfeiffer Rd, Woodside SA 5244
   Ph: (08) 8389 9488
   www.birdinhand.com.au

6. **Bremerton Wines** PAGE 93
   Strathalbyn Rd,
   Langhorne Creek SA 5255
   Ph: (08) 8537 3093
   www.bremerton.com.au

7. **Burge Family Winemakers** PAGE 27
   Barossa Valley Way, Lyndoch SA 5351
   Ph: (08) 8524 4644
   www.burgefamily.com.au

8. **Cape Jaffa Wines** PAGE 66
   Limestone Coast Rd,
   Mount Benson SA 5275
   Ph: (08) 8768 5053
   www.capejaffawines.com.au

9. **Chain of Ponds Winery** PAGE 15
   198c Torrens Valley Rd,
   Gumeracha SA 5233
   Ph: (08) 8389 1901
   www.chainofponds.com.au

10. **Chapman River Wines** PAGE 14
    73 Allan Lashmar Rd,
    Antechamber Bay,
    Kangaroo Island SA 5222
    Ph: (08) 8553 1371

11. **Charles Melton Wines** PAGE 67
    Krondorf Rd, Tanunda SA 5352
    Ph: (08) 8563 3606
    www.charlesmeltonwines.com.au

12. **Coriole Vineyards** PAGE 96
    Chaffeys Rd, McLaren Vale SA 5171
    Ph: (08) 8323 8305
    www.coriole.com

13. **Doc Adams Wines** PAGE 181
    41 High St, Willunga SA 5172
    Ph: (08) 8556 2111
    www.docadamswines.com.au

14. **Dudley Wines** PAGE 99
    1153 Willoughby Rd, Penneshaw,
    Kangaroo Island SA 5222
    Ph: (08) 8553 1333
    www.dudleywines.com.au

15. **Eldredge Vineyards** PAGE 97
    Spring Valley Rd, Clare SA 5453
    Ph: (08) 8842 3086
    www.eldredge.com.au

16. **Fox Creek Wines** PAGE 84
    90 Malpas Rd, McLaren Vale SA 5171
    Ph: (08) 8557 0000
    www.foxcreekwines.com

17. **Graham Stevens Wines** PAGE 52
    72 Ingoldby Rd, McLaren Flat SA 5171
    Ph: (08) 8383 0997
    www.grahamstevenswines.com.au

18. **Greg Cooley Wines** PAGE 29
    Lot 1, Main North Rd, Clare SA 5453
    Ph: (08) 8843 4284
    www.gregcooleywines.com.au

19. **Henschke Cellars** PAGE 53
    1428 Keyneton Rd, Keyneton SA 5353
    Ph: (08) 8564 8223
    www.henschke.com.au

20. **Heritage Wines** PAGE 147
    106a Seppeltsfield Rd,
    Marananga SA 5355
    Ph: (08) 8562 2880
    www.heritagewinery.com.au

21. **Hugh Hamilton Wines** PAGE 101
    McMurtrie Rd, McLaren Vale SA 5171
    Ph: (08) 8323 8689
    www.hughhamiltonwines.com.au

22. **Jenke Vineyards** PAGE 106
    Barossa Valley Way,
    Rowland Flat SA 5352
    Ph: (08) 8524 4154
    www.jenke-vineyards.com

23. **Jim Barry Wines** PAGE 109
    Craig Hill Rd, Clare SA 5453
    Ph: (08) 8842 2261
    www.jimbarry.com

24. **Kellermeister** PAGE 146
    Barossa Valley Way, Lyndoch SA 5351
    Ph: (08) 8524 4303
    www.kellermeister.com.au

25. **Kersbrook Hill Wines** PAGE 17
    1498 South Para Rd, Kersbrook SA 5231
    Ph: (08) 8389 3301
    www.kersbrookhill.com.au

26. **Koonara Wines** PAGE 152
    44 Church St, Penola SA 5277
    Ph: (08) 8737 3222
    www.koonara.com

27. **Lake Breezes** PAGES 149, 236
    Step Rd, Langhorne Creek SA 5255
    Ph: (08) 8537 3017
    www.lakebreeze.com.au

28. **Langmeil Winery** PAGE 148
Cnr Para and Langmeil Rds,
Tanunda SA 5352
Ph: (08) 8563 2595
www.langmeilwinery.com.au

29. **Lobethal Road Wines** PAGE 150
Lot 1 Lobethal – Mt Torrens Rd,
Mt Torrens SA 5244
Ph: (08) 8389 4595
www.lobethalroad.com

30. **Malcolm Creek Winery** PAGE 173
33 Bonython Rd, Kersbrook SA 5231
Ph: (08) 8389 3619
www.malcolmcreekwines.com.au

31. **Maverick Wines** PAGE 156
Lot 141, Light Pass Rd, Vine Vale,
Moorooroo, Barossa Valley SA 5352
Ph: (08) 8563 3551
www.maverickwines.com.au

32. **Maxwell Wines** PAGE 172
1 Olivers Rd, McLaren Vale SA 5171
Ph: (08) 8323 8200
www.maxwellwines.com.au

33. **Mt Lofty Ranges** PAGE 28
166 Harris Rd, Lenswood SA 5240
Ph: (08) 8389 8339
www.mtloftyrangesvineyard.com.au

34. **Murray Street Vineyards** PAGES 12, 13
Murray St, Greenock SA 5360
Ph: (08) 8562 8373
www.murraystreet.com.au

35. **Oliver's Taranga** PAGE 212
246 Seaview Rd, McLaren Vale SA 5171
Ph: (08) 8323 8498
www.oliverstaranga.com

36. **Redman Wines** PAGE 69
14830 Riddoch Hwy, Coonawarra SA 5263
Ph: (08) 8736 3331
www.redman.com.au

37. **RockBare Cellar Door** PAGES 4, 70
102 Main St, Hahndorf SA 5245
Ph: (08) 8388 7522
www.rockbare.com.au

38. **Rymill Coonawarra** PAGE 16
Riddoch Hwy, Coonawarra SA 5263
Ph: (08) 8736 5001
www.rymill.com.au

39. **Samuel's Gorge** PAGE 76
193 Chaffeys Rd, McLaren Vale SA 5171
Ph: (08) 8323 8651
www.gorge.com.au

40. **Seppeltsfield Wines** PAGE 36
PMB1, Seppeltsfield Rd,
Seppeltsfield SA 5355
Ph: (08) 8568 6200
www.seppeltsfield.com.au

41. **Shottesbrooke Vineyards** PAGE 214
101 Bagshaws Rd, McLaren Flat SA 5171
Ph: (08) 8383 0002
www.shottesbrooke.com.au

42. **Simpatico Wines** PAGE 215
Cnr Barossa Valley Way and
Vine Vale Rd, Tanunda SA 5355
Ph: (08) 8561 1222
www.simpaticowines.com.au

43. **Stone Bridge Wines** PAGES 160, 161
Gillentown Rd, Clare SA 5453
Ph: (08) 8843 4143
www.stonebridgewines.com.au

44. **Taste Eden Valley Regional Wine Room** PAGE 209
6–8 Washington St, Angaston SA 5353
Ph: (08) 8564 2435
www.tasteedenvalley.com.au

45. **Tim Adams Wines** PAGE 208
Warenda Rd, Clare SA 5433
Ph: (08) 8842 2429
www.timadamswines.com.au

46. **Torbreck Vintners** PAGE 38
Roennfeldt Rd, Marananga SA 5355
Ph: (08) 8562 4155
www.torbreck.com

47. **Turkey Flat Vineyards** PAGE 34
Bethany Rd, Tanunda SA 5352
Ph: (08) 8563 2851
www.turkeyflat.com.au

48. **Wangolina Station** PAGE 32
Cnr Limestone Coast Rd and Southern
Ports Hwy, Mt Benson SA 5275
Ph: (08) 8768 6187
www.wangolina.com.au

49. **Westlake Vineyards** PAGE 223
Diagonal Rd, Ebenezer SA 5355
Ph: 0428 656 208
www.westlakevineyards.com.au

50. **Whistler Wines** PAGES 30, 31
Seppeltsfield Rd, Marananga SA 5355
Ph: (08) 8562 4942
www.whistlerwines.com

51. **Wirra Wirra Vineyards** PAGE 33
McMurtrie Rd, McLaren Vale SA 5171
Ph: (08) 8323 8414
www.wirrawirra.com

WINERY AND VINEYARD LISTINGS: TASMANIA

TASMANIA

1. **Elmslie Wines** PAGE 187
   2 Upper McEwans Rd, Legana TAS 7277
   Ph: (03) 6330 1225
   www.elmsliewines.com.au

2. **Holm Oak Vineyards** PAGES 88, 91
   11 West Bay Rd, Rowella TAS 7270
   Ph: (03) 6394 7577
   www.holmoakvineyards.com.au

3. **Moores Hill Estate** PAGE 175
   3343 West Tamar Hwy,
   Sidmouth TAS 7270
   Ph: (03) 6394 7649
   www.mooreshill.com.au

4. **Moorilla** PAGES 178, 230
   655 Main Rd, Berridale TAS 7011
   Ph: (03) 6277 9900
   www.moorilla.com.au

5. **Three Wishes Vineyard** PAGE 221
   655 Craigburn Rd, Hillwood TAS 7252
   Ph: 0488 948 330
   www.threewishesvineyard.com.au

6. **Winter Brook Vineyard** PAGE 210
   150 Hjorts Rd, Loira TAS 7275
   Ph: (03) 6394 7071
   www.winterbrookvineyard.com.au

WINERY AND VINEYARD LISTINGS: VICTORIA

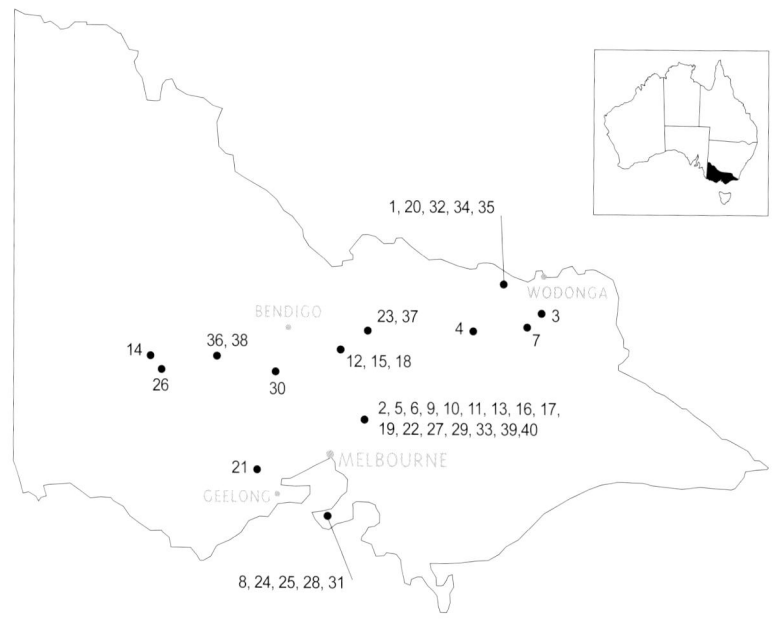

VICTORIA

1. **All Saints Estate** PAGE 25
   All Saints Rd, Wahgunyah VIC 3687
   Ph: (02) 6035 2222
   www.allsaintswine.com.au

2. **Boat O'Craigo** PAGE 92
   458 Maroondah Hwy,
   Healesville VIC 3777
   Ph: (03) 5962 6899
   www.boatocraigo.com.au

3. **Boynton's Feathertop Winery**
   PAGE 50
   6619 Great Alpine Rd,
   Porepunkah VIC 3741
   Ph: (03) 5756 2356
   www.boynton.com.au

4. **Brown Brothers** PAGE 213
   239 Milawa Bobinawarrah Rd,
   Milawa VIC 3678
   Ph: (03) 5720 5500
   www.brownbrothers.com.au

5. **Bulong Estate** PAGE 87
   70 Summerhill Rd,
   Yarra Junction VIC 3797
   Ph: (03) 5967 1358
   www.bulongestate.com.au

6. **Coldstream Hills** PAGE 77
   31 Maddens Lane, Coldstream VIC 3770
   Ph: (03) 5960 7000
   www.coldstreamhills.com

7. **Dal Zotto Wines** PAGE 200
   4861 Wangaratta-Whitfield Rd,
   Whitfield VIC 3733
   Ph: (03) 5729 8321
   www.dalzotto.com.au

8. **Darling Park Winery** PAGE 201
   232 Red Hill Rd, Red Hill VIC 3937
   Ph: (03) 5989 2324
   www.darlingparkwinery.com

9. **De Bortoli Wines (Yarra Valley)**
   PAGE 231
   58 Pinnacle Lane,
   Dixons Creek VIC 3775
   Ph: (03) 5965 2271
   www.debortoli.com.au

10. **Domaine Chandon** PAGES 184, 185
    727 Maroondah Hwy,
    Coldstream VIC 3770
    Ph: (03) 9738 9200
    www.domainechandon.com.au

WINERY AND VINEYARD LISTINGS: VICTORIA

11. **Dominique Portet** PAGE 51
    870 Maroondah Hwy,
    Coldstream VIC 3770
    Ph: (03) 5962 5760
    www.dominiqueportet.com

12. **Flynns Wines** PAGE 154
    Lewis Rd, Heathcote VIC 3523
    Ph: (03) 5433 6297
    www.flynnswines.com

13. **Giant Steps / Innocent Bystander**
    PAGE 110
    336 Maroondah Hwy,
    Healesville VIC 3777
    Ph: (03) 5962 6111
    www.innocentbystander.com.au

14. **Grampians Estate** PAGES 48, 49
    1477 Western Hwy,
    Great Western VIC 3377
    Ph: (03) 5354 6245
    www.grampiansestate.com.au

15. **Heathcote Winery** PAGE 192
    185 High St, Heathcote VIC 3523
    Ph: (03) 5433 2595
    www.heathcotewinery.com.au

16. **Helen's Hill Estate** PAGE 155
    16 Ingram Rd, Coldstream VIC 3770
    Ph: (03) 9737 1573
    www.helenshill.com.au

17. **Immerse in the Yarra Valley** PAGE 102
    1548 Melba Hwy, Dixons Creek VIC 3775
    Ph: (03) 5965 2444
    www.immerse.com.au

18. **Jasper Hill Vineyard** PAGE 202
    88 Drummonds Lane,
    Heathcote VIC 3523
    Ph: (03) 5433 2528
    www.jasperhill.com.au

19. **Killara Estate** PAGE 205
    Cnr Warburton Hwy and Sunnyside Rd,
    Seville East VIC 3139
    Ph: (03) 5961 5877
    www.killaraestate.com.au

20. **Lake Moodemere Vineyards** PAGE 168
    McDonalds Rd, Rutherglen VIC 3685
    Ph: (02) 6032 9449
    www.moodemerewines.com.au

21. **Lethbridge Wines** PAGE 207
    74 Burrows Rd, Lethbridge VIC 3332
    Ph: (03) 5281 7279
    www.lethbridgewines.com

22. **Mandala Wines** PAGE 203
    1568 Melba Hwy, Dixons Creek VIC 3775
    Ph: (03) 5965 2016
    www.mandalawines.com.au

23. **Mitchelton Wines** PAGE 56
    470 Mitchellstown Rd,
    Nagambie VIC 3608
    Ph: (03) 5736 2221
    www.mitchelton.com.au

24. **Moorooduc Estate** PAGES 188–190
    501 Derril Rd, Moorooduc VIC 3933
    Ph: (03) 5971 8506
    www.moorooducestate.com.au

25. **Morning Sun Vineyard** PAGE 199
    337 Main Creek Rd,
    Main Ridge VIC 3928
    Ph: (03) 5989 6571
    www.morningsunvineyard.com.au

26. **Mount Langi Ghiran** PAGE 220
    Vine Rd, Bayindeen VIC 3375
    Ph: (03) 5354 3207
    www.langi.com.au

27. **Mrs Nicks Vineyard** PAGE 206
    238 Myers Rd, Balnarring VIC 3926
    Ph: (03) 5989 7507
    www.mrsnicks.com.au

28. **Nazaaray Estate Winery** PAGES 20, 232
    266 Meakins Rd, Flinders VIC 3929
    Ph: (03) 5989 0126
    www.nazaaray.com.au

29. **Oakridge Wines** PAGE 153
    864 Maroondah Hwy,
    Coldstream VIC 3770
    Ph: (03) 9738 9900
    www.oakridgewines.com.au

30. **Passing Clouds** PAGE 174
    30 Roddas Lane, Musk VIC 3461
    Ph: (03) 5348 5550
    www.passingclouds.com.au

31. **Paynes Rise Winery** PAGE 105
    10 Paynes Rd, Seville VIC 3139
    Ph: (03) 5964 2504
    www.paynesrise.com.au

32. **Scion Vineyard & Winery** PAGES 44, 45
    74 Slaughterhouse Rd,
    Rutherglen VIC 3685
    Ph: (02) 6032 8844
    www.scionvineyard.com

33. **Soumah of Yarra Valley** PAGE 111
    18 Hexham Rd, Gruyere VIC 3770
    Ph: (03) 5962 4716
    www.soumah.com.au

34. **St Leonards Vineyard** PAGE 57
    201 St Leonards Rd,
    Wahgunyah VIC 3687
    Ph: (02) 6035 2222
    www.stleonardswine.com.au

35. **Stanton and Killeen Wines** PAGE 83
    440 Jacks Rd, Rutherglen VIC 3685
    Ph: (02) 6032 9457
    www.stantonandkilleenwines.com.au

36. **Summerfield Wines** PAGE 61
    5967 Stawell Avoca Rd,
    Moonambel VIC 3478
    Ph: (03) 5467 2264
    www.summerfieldwines.com

37. **Tahbilk Wines** PAGES 18, 19
    254 O'Neils Rd,
    Tabilk via Nagambie VIC 3607
    Ph: (03) 5794 2555
    www.tahbilk.com.au

38. **Taltarni Vineyards** PAGE 104
    339 Taltarni Rd, Moonambel VIC 3478
    Ph: (03) 5459 7900
    www.taltarni.com.au

39. **Yarra Yering** PAGE 227
    4 Briarty Rd, Gruyere VIC 3770
    Ph: (03) 5964 9267
    www.yarrayering.com

40. **Yering Station** PAGE 216
    38 Melba Hwy, Yarra Glen VIC 3775
    Ph: (03) 9730 0100
    www.yering.com

WINERY AND VINEYARD LISTINGS: WESTERN AUSTRALIA

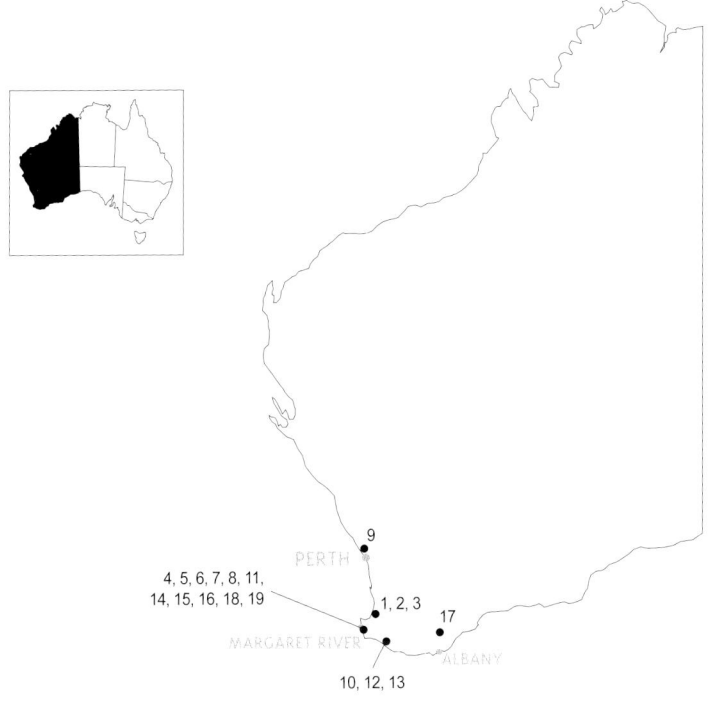

WESTERN AUSTRALIA

1. **Barton Jones Wines** PAGE 79
   39 Upper Capel Rd,
   Donnybrook WA 6239
   Ph: (08) 9731 2233
   www.bartonjoneswines.com.au

2. **Bonking Frog Wines** PAGE 81
   7 Dardanup West Rd,
   North Boyanup WA 6237
   Ph: (08) 9731 5137
   www.bonkingfrog.com.au

3. **Brookhampton Estate** PAGE 58
   19018 South Western Hwy,
   Donnybrook WA 6239
   Ph: (08) 9731 0400
   www.brookhamptonestate.com.au

4. **Brookwood Estate** PAGE 98
   430 Treeton Rd, Cowaramup WA 6284
   Ph: (08) 9755 5604
   www.brookwood.com.au

5. **Cape Naturaliste Vineyard** PAGE 26
   1 Coley Rd, Yallingup WA 6282
   Ph: (08) 9755 2538
   www.capenaturalistevineyard.com.au

6. **Coward & Black at Providore**
   PAGES 64, 65
   448 Harmans South Rd,
   Wilyabrup WA 6280
   Ph: (08) 9755 6355
   www.cowardandblack.com.au

7. **Fermoy Estate** PAGES 176, 177
   838 Metricup Rd, Wilyabrup WA 6284
   Ph: (08) 9755 6285
   www.fermoy.com.au

8. **Flying Fish Cove** PAGE 39
   Lot 125, Caves Rd, Wilyabrup WA 6280
   Ph: (08) 9755 6600
   www.flyingfishcove.com.au

9. **Heafod Glen Winery** PAGE 85
   8691 West Swan Rd,
   Henley Brook WA 6055
   Ph: (08) 9296 3444
   www.heafodglenwine.com.au

10. **Hidden River Estate** PAGE 100
    2 Mullineaux Rd, Pemberton WA 6260
    Ph: (08) 9776 1437
    www.hiddenriver.com.au

11. **Juniper Estate** PAGE 228
    98 Tom Cullity Drive,
    Cowaramup WA 6284
    Ph: (08) 9755 9000
    www.juniperestate.com.au

12. **Lost Lake Wines** PAGE 170
    14591 Vasse Hwy, Pemberton WA 6260
    Ph: (08) 9776 1251
    www.lostlake.com.au

13. **Salitage Winery** PAGE 165
    14429 Vasse Hwy, Pemberton WA 6260
    Ph: (08) 9776 1771
    www.salitage.com

14. **Saracen Estates** PAGES 10, 11
    3517 Caves Rd, Wilyabrup WA 6285
    Ph: (08) 9755 6000
    www.saracenestates.com.au

15. **Vasse Felix** PAGE 164
    Cnr Tom Cullity Drive and Caves Rd
    Cowaramup WA 6284
    Ph: (08) 9756 5000
    www.vassefelix.com.au

16. **Voyager Estate** PAGES 6, 116–141
    Stevens Rd, Margaret River WA 6285
    Ph: (08) 9757 6354
    www.voyagerestate.com.au

17. **West Cape Howe Wines** PAGES 162, 163
    14923 Muir Hwy, Mount Barker WA 6324
    Ph: (08) 9892 1444
    www.westcapehowewines.com.au

18. **Wills Domain** PAGE 226
    Brash Rd, Yallingup WA 6282
    Ph: (08) 9755 2327
    www.willsdomain.com.au

19. **Woodlands Wines** PAGE 211
    3984 Caves Rd, Wilyabrup WA 6284
    Ph: (08) 9755 6226
    www.woodlandswines.com

WINE DOGS BREED INDEX

A
Australian Bulldog PAGES 17, 200
Australian Shepherd PAGES 21, 32, 84
Australian Silky Terrier X PAGE 187

B
Beagle PAGES 44, 218
Bernese Mountain Dog PAGE 223
Bloodhound PAGE 196
Blue Heeler PAGES 16, 171, 215
Blue Heeler X PAGES 82, 134, 163
Border Collie PAGES 4, 25, 30, 37, 49, 70, 74, 83, 93, 138, 149, 181, 206, 210, 211, 226, 229, 236, 253
Border Collie X PAGES 162, 183
Border Terrier PAGE 207
Boxer PAGES 27, 106
Boxer X PAGE 47
Bull Arab PAGE 117
Bull Arab X PAGES 22, 151

C
Cairn Terrier PAGE 111
Cattle Dog PAGES 63, 95
Cavalier King Charles Spaniel PAGE 15
Chihuahua PAGES 136, 146
Cocker Spaniel PAGE 85
Corgi, Pembroke PAGE 139
Curly-Coated Retriever PAGES 99, 101

D
Dachshund, Miniature PAGES 53, 58
Dalmatian PAGES 67, 121, 169
Dingo X PAGE 79

F
Fox Terrier PAGE 142
Fox Terrier X PAGE 150
French Bulldog PAGES 40, 109

G
German Shepherd PAGE 57
German Shorthaired Pointer PAGES 36, 51, 172, 176, 185, 186, 202
Golden Retriever PAGES 64, 65, 102, 103, 209
Golden Retriever X PAGE 118
Greyhound PAGE 29
Greyhound X PAGE 81
Groodle PAGE 208
Groodle, Miniature PAGES 52, 116

H
Heeler X PAGE 104
Hungarian Vizsla PAGES 46, 148, 178, 230
Huntaway X PAGE 13

I
Italian Greyhound X PAGE 55

J
Jack Russell Terrier PAGES 1, 14, 24, 26, 27, 54, 55, 61, 69, 100, 122, 132, 156, 165, 168, 191, 227
Jack Russell Terrier X PAGES 12, 48, 152, 225

K
Kangaroo, Western Grey PAGE 31
Kelpie PAGES 38, 49, 68, 99, 130, 154, 161, 173, 174, 192
Kelpie X PAGES 6, 19, 34, 58, 62, 105, 131, 138, 140, 176, 204, 228

L
Labradoodle PAGES 18, 182
Labrador PAGES 20, 28, 33, 60, 78, 80, 82, 87, 110, 125, 126, 127, 137, 147, 155, 165, 170, 184, 203, 211, 215, 216, 224, 231, 232
Labrador X PAGES 59, 97, 98, 118, 185, 213

M
Maltelier PAGE 136
Maltese X PAGES 50, 86, 97, 128, 129, 199
Maremma PAGE 66
Mixed PAGE 112
Moodle PAGE 166

N
Newfoundland PAGE 11

O
Old English Sheepdog X PAGE 26

P
Parrot, Alexandrian PAGE 119
Pig PAGES 88, 91
Poodle PAGES 56, 188
Poodle, Miniature PAGES 189, 190, 198, 207, 222
Poodle, Standard PAGE 188
Poodle, Toy PAGE 201
Pug PAGES 39, 75

R
Rhodesian Ridgeback PAGES 107, 123, 178, 214
Rhodesian Ridgeback X PAGES 45, 124, 133, 212
Rottweiler PAGE 197
Rottweiler X PAGE 92

S
Saint Bernard PAGE 205
Schnauzer PAGE 141
Shar Pei PAGE 120
Shih Tzu X PAGE 35, 126
Siberian Husky PAGE 77
Staffordshire Terrier PAGES 10, 23, 94, 153, 164, 167, 177
Staffordshire Terrier X PAGES 160, 210, 221

T
Tenterfield Terrier PAGES 96, 108, 119
Terrier X PAGE 220

W
Weimaraner PAGE 175
Weimaraner, Long-haired PAGE 76
West Highland Terrier PAGE 135

THANK YOU...

Wine Dogs would like to thank the following people who helped us on our journey.

Thanks to Peter 'Rock Giant' Herring, Huon Hooke, Norm, Pat, Jim and Isobel for all their support, Jennifer Grieve from Wine Dogs Italy, Emma 'tweet queen' Moroney, Vicki Wild and Martin Benn from Sepia Restaurant & Wine Bar, Robert and Vanessa Martin and the gang from Australia's premier Italian restaurant – Il Piave. We also have a fabulous network of friends (too many to mention), whose constant support and help have made this book a lot easier to produce.

The production of this title was made more difficult by the loss of our last two beloved huskies. The 18-year legacy that our three huskies, Tok, Tarka and Stella have left us will always be treasured. We miss them every day.

Along our travels we were helped and encouraged by many wonderful people, including Peter and Margaret Lehmann, Pam O'Donnell at Rockford Wines, Sean Blocksidge from The Margaret River Discovery Company, Eliza Brown at All Saints Estate, Dave Powell at Torbreck Vintners, PJ Charteris and Chrissi Pattison, Marshy and Holly Marsh at Marsh Estate, Damian Shaw at Philip Shaw, Jim Chatto at Pepper Tree Wines, Jon Osbeiston at Ultimo Wine Centre, Janine Hallas at Yarra Yering and Cindy Talmadge at Murray's Brewing Co.

When staying in the Barossa, Wine Dogs chooses to stay at the fantastic Belle Escapes cottages, located conveniently in the heart of the Barossa and only staggering distance from all your favourite cellar doors.

When in the Hunter Valley, Wine Dogs chooses to stay at Wandin Valley Estate in the greener pastures of Lovedale in the Lower Hunter Valley. The beautiful self-contained villas are set amongst the vines and are conveniently located at the gateway of the Hunter wine country – enjoy the great wine as you explore this unique estate.

In Tasmania, Wine Dogs chooses to stay at MONA Pavilions, which provide contemporary-designed sophisticated accommodation on Moorilla Estate in Hobart. Surrounded by amazing art, food, wine and beer – does it get any better than this?

We would like to express our gratitude to all the wineries that gifted us with some of the most superb wines you could ever taste.

And we must draw special attention to the generosity and hospitality offered to us by Voyager Estate in the Margaret River. We really appreciate all their support of Wine Dogs. This distinguished winery is truly one of the great wine estates of the world.

Special thanks to all our contributors: Nick Ryan, Nick Stock, Greg Duncan Powell, Ben Canaider, Peter Forrestal, Tory Shepherd, Andrew Marsh, Matthew Jukes, Emma Moroney and Tyson Stelzer for their excellently crafted stories and support. Thanks guys.

To Catherine 'Demon' Rendell for her amazing Wine Dogs website work, Lily Li and Vicky Fisher for helping make Wine Dogs better every year.

Our apologies to the wineries that we didn't visit. Please contact us for entry into the next edition.

WINE DOGS AUSTRALIA 4: If your winery and woofer missed out on appearing in this edition, please contact us at entries@winedogs.com and register for the Wine Dogs Australia 4. We'll look forward to hearing from you. Woof!

IN MEMORY OF ALL OUR BELOVED WINE DOGS